# Cape Cod

# Glass Dinnerware

## 2nd Edition

Debbie and Randy Coe

4880 Lower Valley Road, Atglen, Pennsylvania 19310

Designed by Bonnie M. Hensley
Cover design by Bruce Waters
Type set in University Roman Bd BT/Dutch 801 Rm BT

ISBN: 978-0-7643-3679-9
Printed in China
1 2 3 4

Published by Schiffer Publishing Ltd.
4880 Lower Valley Road
Atglen, PA 19310
Phone: (610) 593-1777; Fax: (610) 593-2002
E-mail: info@schifferbooks.com
Please visit our web site catalog at **www.schifferbooks.com**
We are always looking for people to write books on new and related subjects. If you have an idea for
a book, please contact us at the above address.

This book may be purchased from the publisher. Include $5.00 for shipping.
Please try your bookstore first. You may write for a free catalog.

In Europe, Schiffer books are distributed by
Bushwood Books
6 Marksbury Ave. Kew Gardens
Surrey TW9 4JF England
Phone: 44 (0)20 8392-8585; Fax: 44 (0)20 8392-9876
E-mail: info@bushwoodbooks.co.uk

Please try your bookstore first.

# Dedication

We dedicate this book to Debbie's mother, Merlyn Stanhurst. When we began collecting Royal Ruby glassware, she thought Avon's Cape Cod would be an excellent addition. We appreciate all the help she has given us to complete our set. She still is a valued Avon Representative, too. We love her lots!

# Acknowledgements

The idea for this book grew out of a casual conversation with our good friend, Donna Miller. She mentioned her awareness of collectors of Avon's Cape Cod, but that only limited information was available about the pattern. Since we had collected the entire pattern, we thought we should share the information we had gathered. Donna and her husband, Ron, also furnished some of the boxes we needed to photograph.

Susan Hansen, at Avon Products, Inc., did her best to furnish information about the pattern. Unfortunately, she wasn't working at Avon during the time it was being made and all the people involved with the project have now left the company. She was gracious and gave us basic information about the 1876 Cape Cod collection.

We knew that the Wheaton Glass Company in Millville, New Jersey, had made the glass, since brochures naming them came with the glass when we originally obtained the pieces. Bob Hill, a friend at the Fenton Glass Company mould shop, furnished some information about Wheaton. Bob had worked at Wheaton in 1964 and 1965, but didn't know if any of his colleagues were still there. Being the helpful guy he is, he suggested asking Don Cunningham, also at Fenton, and he put us in contact with Curtis Zimmerman, at Wheaton.

Curtis Zimmerman, a Group Leader and Senior Technician at Wheaton Glass, was happy to give us assistance. Curtis has been at Wheaton for 37 years and was working there during the entire time the 1876 Cape Cod pattern was produced. He answered all of our many questions and gladly referred us to another long-time employee, Everett Chance.

A designer for Wheaton, Everett Chance has been working at Wheaton for 41 years and was also a fantastic source of information. He miraculously located a few sample pieces and made them available to be photographed. He really went out of his way to locate information we thought was essential for this book. He located and obtained permission for us to include original mould drawings for most of the glass pieces. The information on the drawings provided the names of the designers and specific measurements. Everett also located production data that included the number of moulds and type of machine used to make each piece. Both Curtis Zimmerman and Everett Chance were gracious to help us. We are very thankful for their help

Bruce Waters, of the Schiffer Publishing staff, photographed the sample pieces and designed the book's cover.

Our daughters, Myra and Tara, have both provided assistance proof reading and giving advice on what to include. Tara and her husband, Jeff, were also a big help in locating original boxes and brochures. We love all three of them very much. Debbie's sister, Diane Wiley, also assisted with getting them more original boxes along with a copy of an older Avon book.

It takes many sources to put together a book and without everyone's willingness to provide us with information, this book would not contain all the facts it does; we are only the instruments in putting all of the facts together. We are indebted to everyone involved.

# Contents

# Introduction

When Avon Products, Inc., best known as a marketer for cosmetics, introduced a new glass dinnerware line, the 1876 Cape Cod Collection, in 1975. This was a departure from their normal sales line. As more glass dinnerware items were made available, new customers became interested in completing a set. By the time the pattern was discontinued in 1993, there were 37 different items in the line. A magnificent table could be set to mark special occasions.

It sometimes takes the event of being discontinued to attract new collectors to a product. People can procrastinate about collecting something when it is always available, but when it is no longer offered, all of a sudden there is an urge to obtain it. As time passed, the Avon 1876 Cape Cod pieces started to show up on the secondary market, enticing new collectors to begin gathering the pieces or providing a chance for people with the set to add more pieces.

The vibrant ruby color is an attraction to the pattern. Low prices for the pieces also gave people a reason to look for this pattern while the pieces were plentiful. Many Depression glass patterns had gotten so expensive and hard to find that new collectors were looking for a reasonably priced pattern. When the 1876 Cape Cod caught their eye, the hunt began.

After several requests from customers, we have added the original selling price on the items. Many of you told us that your insurance companies had requested these prices when settling a claim. In our opinion, past prices paid have nothing to do with the value today. Current economic conditions will dictate what an item is worth and all we can do is supply the sustainable values we find on the marketplace.

In this new edition we have also pictured a few more items with their original boxes. A new last chapter is the addition of the newly found table runner and napkin kits. These were offered at the end of the Cape Cod promotion and gave you an opportunity to apply your embroidery skills to have a coordinating item for your table.

## Measurements

All measurements given are actual sizes. Bowls, butter dish, candy dish, ornament, plates, platter and saucer are measured according to their diameter or length, whether they are round or oblong. Creamer, cup, mug, and pitcher are measured by height and liquid measurement is given in ounces. Shakers are measured by height only.

## Value Guide

Values are given for MINT CONDITION only! Items that are chipped or scratched bring substantially less than the given price. Since this is a new collectible area, any item that is cracked has no value. Bowls are especially susceptible to chipping on the inside edge because they often are stacked. Some people want to collect the original boxes, too; therefore, we give values for items with their boxes.

There are, of course, differences in the prices across the different regions. Some pieces may be more prevalent in different areas. In general, dinner plates and serving pieces are the most sought after items in this pattern.

Prices on the internet tend to be lower than ones found at a show or shop, due to the weight of each of the items. This glass is quite heavy for its size and they cost more to ship. The bidder takes in consideration the cost of the shipping when bidding on the item. For instance, a dinner plate valued at $19.50 may cost around $10 to ship, so the winning bid may only come in around $8 or $9. No one is happy with the decline in value of their items, but it is no different than the reduction in value on a house, investments or retirement accounts. The bright side is that lower prices are attracting new collectors and that in turn will eventually cause the items to go back up in value.

The values stated here have been derived from several sources. Remember, the ultimate decision on value rests with the collector who decides what they are willing to pay for an item. Neither the authors nor the publisher assume responsibility for transactions that may occur because of this book.

# Background of Avon Products Company and the 1876 Cape Cod Collection

David McConnell left the family farm in 1878 in search of a better life. His first job was as a door-to-door book salesman. After several promotions, David purchased the entire book-selling business.

Upon becoming the boss, David concentrated on how to better serve his customers. While investigating several possibilities, David also looked at other types of products that could be sold door-to-door. His women customers told him they wanted good quality perfumes at a reasonable price.

David and his wife started developing natural perfumes in their kitchen, to sell to their book customers. Soon the perfume sales were far outnumbering the book sales and the decision was made to start a new company. But what should they call it? A close friend of theirs had just moved to California at this time, and he wrote to the McConnell's how beautiful it was there. With thoughts of their friend, the California Perfume Company was ironically established in Suffern, New York, in 1886.

The perfume line was expanded and many other personal care items were developed. Women customers greatly valued the convenience of fine products being brought directly to their doors.

As sales increased, the company expanded by adding more laboratories to develop new products. One of these new laboratories was located in Avon, England. Since the area resembled Suffern, New York, a new line of products called Avon was introduced in 1928, to honor that community.

The company's name was officially changed in 1939 to Avon Products, Inc. During the Second World War, the company added to its lines insect repellents and medicines for people to send to their military family members. By 1949, Avon sold $25 million worth of products and had distribution facilities in New York, Kansas City, Chicago, and Pasadena.

During the 1960s, Avon Products commissioned the Wheaton Glass Company in Millville, New Jersey, to make decorative decanters for Avon to sell. Car decanters were introduced in 1968 and became Avon's most successful type of decanter. The plastic colored lids were made at the Wheaton plastics division. Specifications on the lids required the colors to match the glass.

Avon Products stock was first traded on the New York Stock Exchange in 1964. Eight years later, in 1972, Avon's new headquarters were finished in New York City and the company moved to this new facility. Sales at that time were over a billion dollars.

Grouping of Avon's 1876 Cape Cod Collection.
**Left to right**: Shaker, dessert plate, elegant wine (claret), dinner plate, hurricane candleholder, cup and saucer.

Avon's 1876 Cape Cod Collection table setting.
**Back Row**: Dessert bowl, shakers, elegant wine (claret), water goblet.
**Front Row**: Dinner plate, napkin ring.

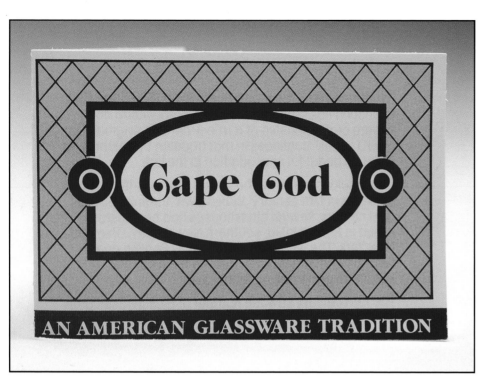

Original 1876 Cape Cod brochure, front view.

For fifteen years the magnificent Avon 1876 Cape Cod Collection has captured the spirit, enthusiasm and superb craftsmanship of a true American original. Our "1990 series" continues in that tradition by celebrating with this beautiful new addition to the line.

Glassmaking began in the United States with the first colonists in 17th century Jamestown, Virginia. By the next century, several glasshouses had been established in Philadelphia, southern New Jersey, Ohio and New York. The workmen were mainly English and German immigrants who drew on the wealth of European glassmaking techniques.

The 19th century saw the number of glasshouses grow from a dozen to nearly one hundred. Machines for pressing glass were constructed in Boston and Cape Cod. The exceptional glass produced by the Boston & Sandwich Glass Works of Cape Cod in particular was the inspiration for the name of this collection.

Avon continues this American tradition by entrusting the production of this fine collection to the Wheaton Glass Company of New Jersey. Wheaton, a family owned and operated business for over a century, has been manufacturing the Cape Cod Collection since 1975.

The Cape Cod Collection is reminiscent of early American "sandwich glass." It recreates the lacy, intricate designs, fine background stippling and expert

Original 1876 Cape Cod brochure, centerfold view.

Original 1876 Cape Cod brochure, back view.

artistry of this singular American art form. This complex, highly skilled production method is modeled after the original hand-blown procedure.

The result is unique and incomparable glassware. As with any fine glassware production, color and surface differences may occur. While each item in the Cape Cod Collection may not precisely replicate others, you'll find that the variations lend an authentic hand-crafted quality to the collection.

TO CLEAN: Wash by hand with mild soap and water, as you would all fine glassware. DO NOT CLEAN IN DISHWASHER.

Avon Products, Inc., New York, N.Y. 10019
©Avon 1990—All Rights Reserved

Sample item of hurricane candleholder base in flint glass (crystal).

Sample item of the saucer champagne in flint glass (crystal).

11

Pattern detail.

Sample item of the water goblet in flint glass (crystal).

## THE 1876 CAPE COD COLLECTION

The condiment dish of the 1876 Cape Cod Collection is reminiscent of early American pressed glass called "Sandwich Glass". It featured lacy, intricate designs, fine background stippling, and exquisite brilliance which reflected the superb craftsmanship of its makers.

Many of the detailed designs of this prized glass were produced by the Boston & Sandwich Glass Works founded on Cape Cod in 1825. Other companies in the region competed, but the popularity of "Sandwich" pieces resulted in the name becoming a generic term for pressed glass.

This unique Avon 1876 Cape Cod Collection was inspired by the classic Roman Rosette pattern. The collection name commemorates both the spirit of the 1876 Philadelphia Centennial, the celebration of the 100th anniversary of the signing of the Declaration of Independence, and, Cape Cod, the area where Sandwich glass originated.

AVON PRODUCTS, INC., DISTR., NEW YORK, N.Y. 10019
©AVON 1985—ALL RIGHTS RESERVED

Close-up of the statement that is on each box. Note: the statement stays the same, except that the name of the item changes from box to box (according to what is in it). For example, this is the box for the divided relish (condiment dish).

Original types of boxes that were used.
**Left:** White and gray box. **Right top:** Red and white with gold box, this style was used most often. **Right bottom:** Red and gold with white box, found to be used only with the cup and saucer.

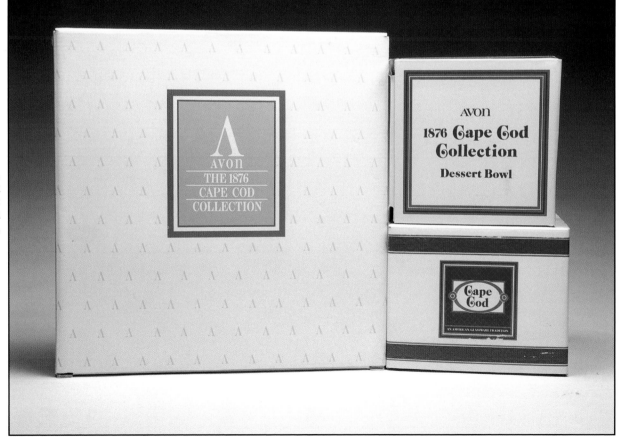

13

An assortment of different sizes of boxes, shown on their side with the name of the item that goes inside.

## Development of the 1876 Cape Cod Collection

During 1974, Avon Products started plans to offer a glass dinnerware line. Since all of the employees involved with this line are now gone from the company, it can only be assumed that Avon was trying to provide a line to commemorate the American Bi-centennial in 1976 and to capture a part of the market held by other door-to-door marketers, Princess House and Tiara. Both of these home-party sales companies offered attractive glass dinnerware sets: Princess House had the Fantasia and Heritage sets and Tiara was selling a Sandwich line.

Avon turned to Wheaton Glass to make a new dinnerware line, and they called it the 1876 Cape Cod Collection. The pattern was based on a nineteenth-century Sandwich Glass design called Roman Rosette. Avon designers made the original concepts that were sent to Wheaton Glass to be evaluated for production. There were about a dozen designers in Wheaton's design department, at the time, and they developed drawings with corrections and additions to the original sketches, based on the size and weight of each proposed glass item. Several people at Wheaton Glass checked over these drawings carefully to make sure they were correct before production began. Modified mould drawings were then sent Avon for final approval.

### Wheaton Glass Designers and Checkers for Avon's 1876 Cape Cod Collection

The following list identifies the designers and checkers who worked on the drawings for the 1876 Cape Cod Collection.

Scott Babbitt (Designer) - still at Wheaton and in Mould Design

Everett Chance (Designer & Checker) - still a Designer at Wheaton

Roy Cramer (Designer) - deceased

Bill Gibson (Designer & Checker) - has left Wheaton and works for another company

Tom Godfrey (Checker) - still at Wheaton and a Design Manager

Ed Magee (Designer & Checker) - has left Wheaton

William Miller (Designer) - retired from Wheaton

Bud Norcross (Designer) - deceased

Bob O'Donnell (Designer) - still at Wheaton and is Director of Product Development

Al Osti (Designer & Checker) - has left Wheaton and works for another company

Bruce Pierce (Designer) - still at Wheaton and in Product Development

Jere Reed (Checker) - retired

Charles Riley (Checker) - retired

A mystery surfaced when going through the production records. Though not a normal business practice, Avon also sent a drawing to the Anchor Hocking Corporation so they could also develop a mould for Avon. Since the Collection was already in production at Wheaton, with a dozen or so items, why they sent a drawing to Anchor Hocking is not known. The exact answer will remain a mystery. We can only go with the written facts in the company records. Designated as the #5738 dessert bowl, Anchor Hocking probably did develop the item for Avon, made the production mould equipment, and possibly did a test run. Avon abruptly instructed Anchor Hocking to send all the moulds and materials involved over to Wheaton Glass. This was unusual for a competitor to receive another company's work. A new development order, dated April 6, 1981, instructed the Wheaton personnel to duplicate a glass sample they had received from Anchor Hocking. A production order was written on September 22, 1981, and an order was sent to the mould shop on September 30, 1981 instructing them to re-register the item from Anchor Hocking #5738 to become Wheaton #AP-54. The mould equipment was then altered to adapt to the Wheaton machines and a run of 275,000 pieces was produced. According to the Avon company records, this was the only item Wheaton received from Anchor Hocking that was re-developed as part of the Cape Cod line. Wheaton Glass designed all other original material for the 1876 Cape Cod Collection.

### The Moulding Processes

Wheaton Glass developed and made the moulds for this new Avon pattern in their mould shop. Approximately 20 moulds were made for each item in production, with four to six moulds held in reserve, in case one needed repairs. The quantity of the production order dictated how many moulds were made. For quality control purposes, each mould, or cavity, was assigned a number. If there was a problem with one of the sections, it could easily be traced by reading the number on the glass item.

There were two methods for making these glass items at Wheaton. Of the 37 pieces produced, five were made on equipment called Emhart Individual Section Glass Forming Machines, or IS Machines for short. They are a combination of five or six smaller machines or sections, each running independently of the others. They utilize a common delivery system for the molten glass and a conveying system for the finished product.

For the 1876 Cape Cod Collection, the machines ran a single gob, or one piece, per cycle from each section. Avon's quality requirements and complexity of the designs required this. The pieces made by this process include:

tall candlesticks
decanter
napkin rings
pitcher
shakers

The majority of the Cape Cod items were made on a 16-mould rotary press machine and have an AP designation in front of the mould number. This machine resembles a carousel with a large circular-looking table with the moulds affixed at the edge in equal intervals. As the table moves, molten glass is poured into the moulds and then pressed into the shape of the mould. The finished product is then put on a common conveyor belt to move it into the annealing, or cooling, kiln. The pieces made by this method are:

bell
all the bowls
trinket box
butter dish
cake plate
gravy boat
hurricane candle holder bottom
short candlestick
candy dish
creamer
cup & saucer
all goblets
mug
ornament
all plates
platter
all tumblers

## The Glass

According to Curtis Zimmerman, Wheaton's group leader and senior technician, a special dense red glass formula was developed exclusively for the 1876 Cape Cod Collection. The specifications from Avon required the glass to be a dark red color upon reheating, with no hint of yellow color in the glass. It was extremely hard to maintain this dark red color, since the glass needs to be reheated to an exact temperature. There could only be slight differences to the red color between the batches. Avon had a color range of what was acceptable to them. This red color was later also used for some of the Avon decanters.

Upon completion of each mould, the items were normally first sampled in flint glass, a clear or crystal glass that contains some lead. The samples were then sent to Avon for approval before production began. Everett Chance, one of Wheaton's designers, related that if Wheaton had red glass in production when the samples were made, the sample could also have been made in that color, too. In cases of transition from one color to the next, samples could have also been produced in odd colors. A few sample blue pieces have been reported.

## Packaging the Collection

When the 1876 Cape Cod Collection was introduced in 1975, the first two pieces were the tall candlesticks and the cruet. The following information was printed on each box.

The 1876 Cape Cod Collection. This (name of the particular boxed item is inserted here) is reminiscent of the early American pressed glass called Sandwich Glass. It featured lacy intricate designs, fine background stippling and exquisite brilliance, which reflected the superb craftsmanship of its makers. Many of the detailed designs of this prized glass were produced by the Boston and Sandwich Glass Works, founded on Cape Cod in 1825. Other companies in the region competed, but the popularity of Sandwich pieces resulted in the name becoming a generic term for pressed glass. Inspired by the lacy delicacy of these designs, particularly the classic Roman Rosette pattern, Avon has created this unique collection. Not only does it recall the beauty of this quality glass, but its name commemorates both the spirit of the 1876 Philadelphia Centennial, which celebrated the 100th Anniversary of the Declaration of Independence and the area where Sandwich glass originated.

The packaging was all designed by Avon Products, Inc. and was contracted out to local paper companies, resulting in three different styles of boxes. The glass was bulk packaged in partitioned cartons at Wheaton and sent to whichever box company Avon directed. (Other items that needed to be filled with a cologne or bubble bath were sent to another location and packaged there.)

## Variations in Design

Initially, the dessert server was scheduled to be made with a glass handle. The metal blade for the server had been contracted to Regent Sheffield of England. A glass handle was supposed to be attached to the metal blade. After numerous unforeseen problems, the knife was sent to the Wheaton plastics division to have the handle made there. This was the only major item from the collection to be made in a plastic. The shaker lids and liner to the decanter stopper were also made in red plastic that matched the glass. The plastic liners for the tall candlestick and cruet were made in a clear plastic.

Avon continued to add new pieces to the collection each year and some items were discontinued. In the last year of production, 1993, the cup & saucer, bread & butter plate, and pie plate were made. During the following couple of years, orders still could be placed for any item still in stock, but no new pieces were made. Gradually, inventory was depleted and, by 1995, the 1876 Cape Cod Collection was officially discontinued.

Susan Hansen from Avon Products says, "there are no plans to bring the 1876 Cape Cod pattern back." By the early 1990s, she said Avon felt it had produced all the possible pieces for this pattern and when sales were declining, the decision was made to discontinue it.

Once production of the 1876 Cape Cod ceased in 1993, the moulds were stored in the Wheaton Glass mould shop. In the years since, Wheaton Glass has undergone several ownership changes. In the summer of 1996, Wheaton was sold to Alusuisse Lonza, a company from Switzerland, and the name of the glass company was changed to Lawson Mardon Wheaton, and later simplified to AL Group Wheaton. In 2000, the company was sold to Alcan Packaging and the glass company's name was changed to Wheaton USA. In 2002, Wheaton USA has been put back on the market again and is awaiting a new owner.

### Care of the Collection

Like all good glass dinnerware patterns, the 1876 Cape Cod should bring many years of continual use if attention is paid to its care. The glass needs to be hand washed with regular dish soap. The glass is not designed to withstand the intense heat of a dishwasher. It is not heat resistant and cannot be used in a conventional oven nor in a microwave oven. When stacking the pieces in a cabinet, make sure a liner (such as a paper plate) is placed between all the bowls and plates to prevent chipping and scratching.

### Hummingbird Crystal Dinnerware

In the mid-1980s, Avon had another glass dinnerware line for their customers to purchase. Called Hummingbird Crystal, it featured a white hummingbird among flowers. The Hummingbird Crystal line had about 15 pieces and was discontinued in 1995. The glass for this collection was imported.

Avon Products also commissioned the Fostoria Glass Company to produce some representative gifts for Avon from Fostoria's Coin Glass line. These were made by adapting the Coin Glass moulds to have Avon symbols on them.

# Avon's 1876 Cape Cod Collection

## Bell

**Bell, Hostess, 6.6" tall**

The hostess bell was designed by Scott Babbit. The Wheaton mould drawing number D-26182C shows that it was drawn on December 20, 1978. The job number assigned to the bell was AP-36L and it was approved for production on May 25, 1979. There were 20 moulds made for this item.

Another mould drawing, number D-25884H, shows that the original plunger was changed to read "Christmas 1979" from saying "1979," on May 5, 1979. To see these marks one must look up inside the bell. Beside the metal support for the bells' chain are the marks. On the regular bell you see AVON, in block letters, and across from it is the date, 1979. On the Christmas bell you see AVON, in block letters, across from it is the date, 1979, and above the date is the word CHRISTMAS, in block letters. This bell was only available for the fall 1979 campaigns. The gold colored metal support for the bells' chain is glued into position and a clear glass ball clapper is at the end.

The overall height is 6.6" tall and 3.5" wide across the bottom opening of the bell. The bell was made from 1979 to 1980.

Bell, hostess, 6.6" tall, marked on the inside "1979" or "Christmas 1979", for 1979 only. **$12.50**
For the one marked Christmas 1979. **$13.50**
Add $1.00 for having the original box.
Original selling price $15.00

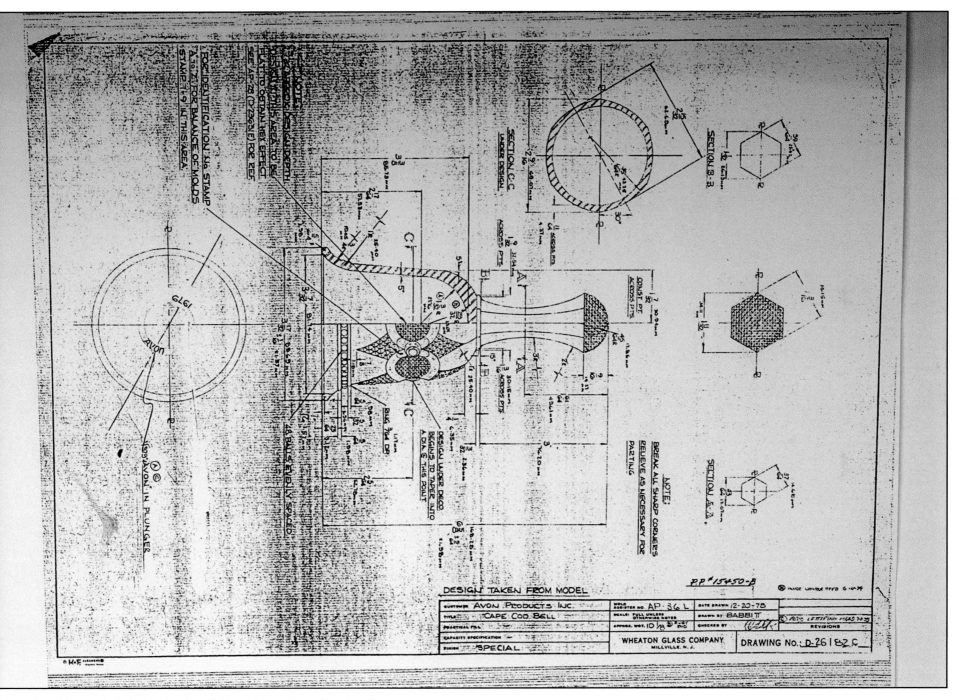

Drawing of hostess bell design showing all dimensions and specifications for production. Marked on inside "1979". *Reprinted with permission from Wheaton USA.*

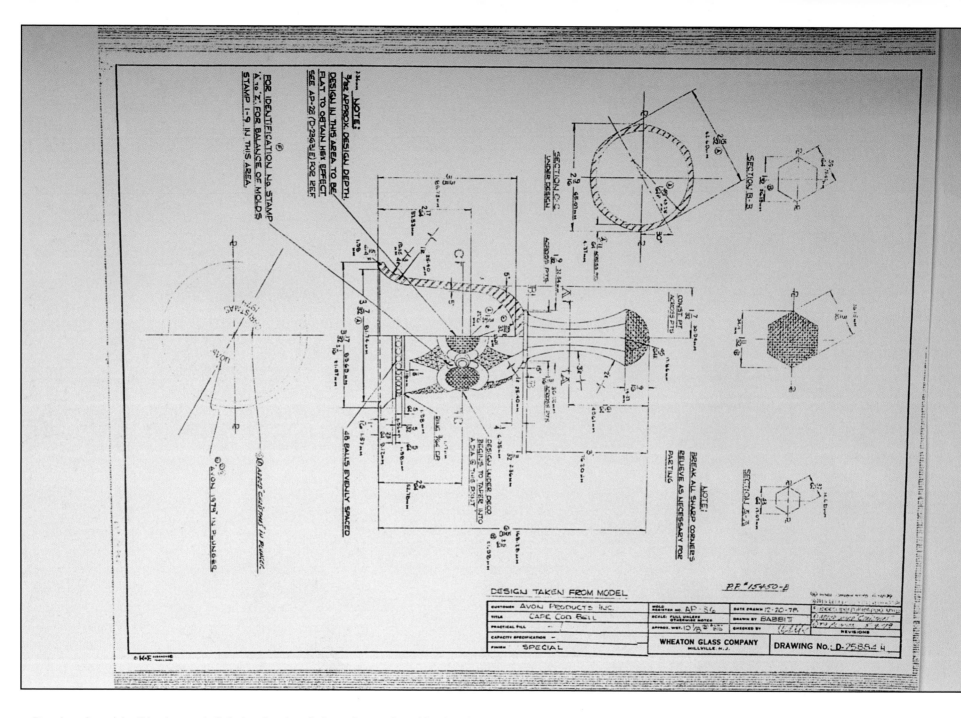

Drawing of special edition hostess bell design showing all dimensions and specifications for production. Marked on inside "Christmas 1979". *Reprinted with permission from Wheaton USA.*

# Bowls

**Dessert Bowl, 5.25" wide**

This is the only item initially developed at Anchor Hocking. It is believed that it was never put into production with Anchor Hocking, but possibly a test run of some dessert bowls could have been made. Avon instructed Anchor Hocking to send the mould equipment for this bowl, #5738, to Wheaton. A new development order at Wheaton on April 6, 1981 called for the mould to be modified to work with their machines. The mould designation number became AP-54, reflecting the mould change. The production order was approved on September 22, 1981.

The bowl was first issued with the bottom marked Avon and the mould number. There were 23 moulds made for this item. The bowl was initially packed by itself.

Later, the backstamp was changed to include the copyright sign © in front of Avon. This modified mould was approved for production on January 10, 1984. This bowl was then packed with three white special occasion soaps.

These bowls are susceptible to chipping around the edge when stacked on top of each other. To prevent this from happening, make sure you put something between them to provide a cushion, such as a napkin.

The bowl is 5.25" wide and is 1.85" tall. The bowl was made from 1981 to 1990.

Comparison photo of bowl sizes. **Top**: Dessert, **Left bottom**: Rim soup, **Right bottom**: Serving bowl (vegetable).

**Dessert bowl, 5.25" wide, 1984 - 1990, $7.50.**
**Left**: Bowl in flat position, **Right**: Bowl in upright position.

Dessert bowl with original box. Boxed price **$8.50**

Detail of backstamp on dessert bowl showing "Avon" and mould number.

Detail of backstamp on dessert bowl showing "© Avon" and mould number.

Dessert bowl with original box and three white special occasion soaps that came with it.
Boxed with soaps price **$9.50. Original selling price $11.00.**

## Rim Soup Bowl, 7.4" wide

The rim soup bowl was approved for production on October 17, 1990 and was given the job number AP-86. There were 31 moulds made for this item.

This was one of the last items to be produced as part of the 1876 Cape Cod Collection. The bowl itself is shallow, with a one-inch flat border.

The bowl is 7.4" wide and 1.5" tall. Production on this bowl was limited to 1991, making it one of the harder pieces to find in the set.

Rim soup bowl, 7.4" wide, 1991, **$14.50**
**Above:** Rim soup bowl with original box. Boxed price $15.50.
**Below:** Rim soup bowl, 7.4" wide, 1991. $14.50. **Left**: Bowl in flat position, **Right**: Bowl in upright position. Add $1.00 for having the original box. **Original selling price $20.00.**

**Serving Bowl, 8.75" wide**

The serving bowl was approved for production on December 11, 1984, but was not made until 1986. Collectors also refer to it as a vegetable bowl. It was assigned job number AP-73 and 18 moulds were made.

**Left**: Original box, **Right**: Serving (vegetable) bowl. Add $2.00 for having the original box.

THE 1876 CAPE COD COLLECTION

The serving bowl of the 1876 Cape Cod Collection is reminiscent of early American pressed glass called "Sandwich Glass". It featured lacy, intricate designs, fine background stippling and exquisite brilliance which reflected the superb craftsmanship of its makers.

Many of the detailed designs of this prized glass were produced by the Boston & Sandwich Glass Works founded on Cape Cod in 1825. Other companies in the region competed, but the popularity of "Sandwich" pieces resulted in the name becoming a generic term for pressed glass.

This unique Avon 1876 Cape Cod Collection was inspired by the classic Roman Rosette pattern. The collection name commemorates both the spirit of the 1876 Philadelphia Centennial, the celebration of the 100th anniversary of the signing of the Declaration of Independence, and, Cape Cod, the area where Sandwich glass originated.

AVON PRODUCTS, INC., DISTR. NEW YORK, N.Y. 10019
© AVON 1986—ALL RIGHTS RESERVED

© AVON

**Opposite page:** Serving (vegetable) bowl, 8.75" wide, 1986-1990, standard issue **$24.50.** Centennial issue **$28.50. Left**: Bowl in flat position. **Right**: Bowl in upright position. Original selling price $18.00.

Detail of backstamp on regular serving (vegetable) bowl.

27

For the first year of production, this was a special issue bowl to coincide with the centennial celebration of Avon. The backstamp reads "Centennial Edition © AVON [in block letters] 1886 – 1986". This Centennial issue was only available in 1986 before the mould was altered. The Centennial bowl also had a special paper brochure included with it describing the Avon celebration. For the rest of the production time, the backstamp on the bowl read © Avon. Since the Centennial issue was made for only one year, it is a little more valuable.

The bowl is 8.75" in diameter and 3" tall. Production of the bowl was from 1986 to 1990.

Original 1876 Cape Cod brochure from special issue Centennial serving (vegetable) bowl - front view.

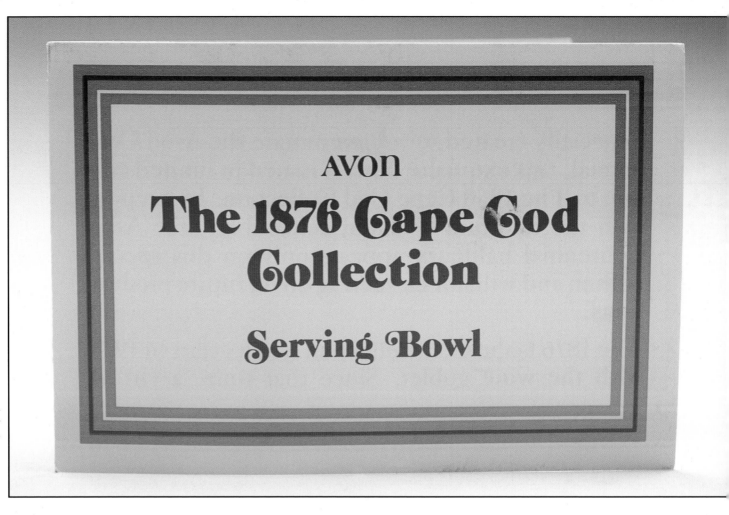

AVON
The 1876 Cape Cod Collection
Serving Bowl

Especially created to commemorate the Avon Centennial, this exquisite bowl is issued in limited edition to The 1876 Cape Cod Collection. In keeping with the tradition of dated collectibles, the Avon Centennial hallmark appears only on this special edition and will not be seen again on future productions.

The 1876 Cape Cod Collection had its start in 1975 with the wine goblet. Since that time, a virtual tableful of distinctive, clear ruby-red glass pieces have been produced. From place settings to serving pieces, the tradition inspired by Early American "Sandwich" glass continues.

And now, more than ten years after the original design appeared, Avon proudly adds this Serving Bowl to the 1876 Cape Cod Collection…the centerpiece of the collection and your home.

Original 1876 Cape Cod brochure from special issue Centennial serving (vegetable) bowl, centerfold view.

Original 1876 Cape Cod brochure from special issue Centennial serving (vegetable bowl), back view.

Detail of backstamp on special issue Centennial serving (vegetable) bowl showing special mark.

# Box

**Heart Trinket Box, 4" wide**

    The heart trinket box was approved for production on April 11, 1988. The box itself was assigned the job number AP-80, while the lid was given the number AP-81. There were 26 moulds made for this piece. This was only one of two covered pieces that were issued in this pattern. The heart box is frequently overlooked, since it is not a typical piece to use on your table. This piece is usually a vanity item. The box is 4" wide, 3.5" long, and 1.4" tall. It was made from 1989 to 1990.

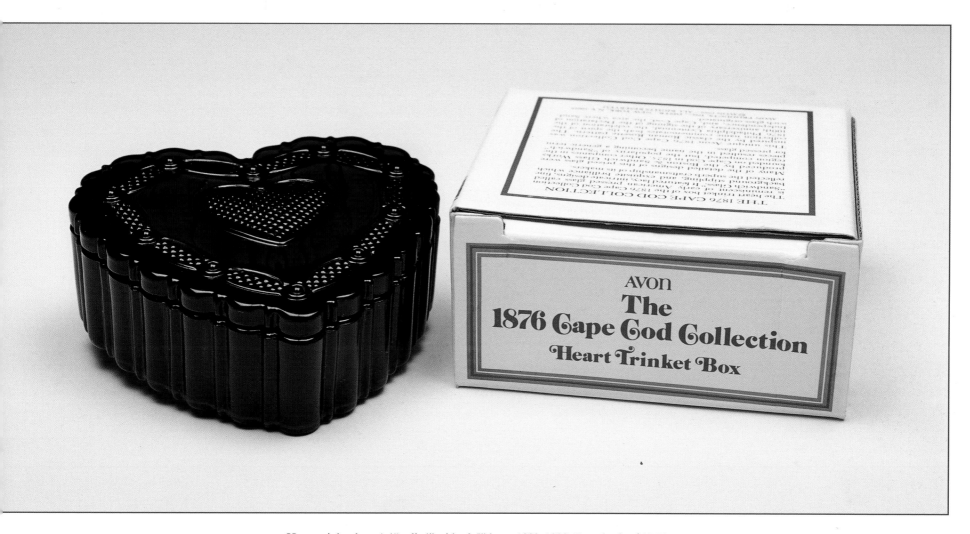

Heart trinket box, 1.4" tall, 4" wide, 3.5" long, 1989, 1990. Boxed price **$13.50**
**Left:** Heart trinket box, **Right**: Original box. Original selling price $9.50.

**Opposite page:** Heart trinket box with lid off and shown in upright position, **$12.50**

# Butter Dish

**Butter Dish, quarter pound, 7" long**

Approval for production of the quarter pound butter dish was made on December 9, 1982. The lid was given the job number AP-59 and the bottom was assigned AP-60. There were 28 moulds made for the lid and 25 moulds for the bottom.

This butter dish held a quarter pound stick of margarine or butter. Besides the trinket box, this was the only other item made with a lid.

The butter dish is 7" long, 3.5" tall, and 3.5" wide. This piece was made from 1983 to 1984.

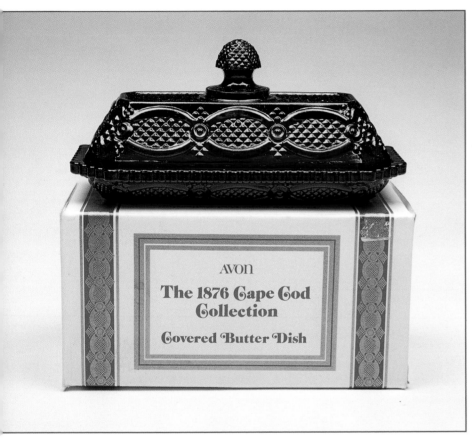

**Top**: Butter dish, **Bottom**: Original box, boxed price **$20.50**

Butter dish with bottom shown in upright position.

**Opposite page:** Butter dish, quarter pound, 3.5" tall, 7" long, 1983-1984, **$19.50.**
**Original selling price $18.50.**

33

# Cake Plate

**Pedestal Cake Plate, 10.75" wide**

The pedestal cake plate was approved for production on May 24, 1991. The cake top was assigned the job number AP-88. The dinner plate was altered to make the cake top. The rays were now on the top and the decorative border was pressed down to form the 1" wide scalloped edge. It resembled the dinner plate, with the bottom rays on top and the decorative border forming the 1" wide scalloped edge. The base, job number AP-89, featured a rayed column with the pattern around the bottom edge. The base resembles the dessert bowl turned upside down. Both of these pieces were produced separately and then put together with an industrial adhesive at the factory. We have had people email us a photo of the top thinking it was a rare item. In fact it is only the top that has separated from the bottom piece. There are some glass repair technicians that are able to glue the two pieces back together if they do become separated. The cake plate is 10.75" wide and 3.5" tall. Year of production was only during 1991, making this piece hard to find.

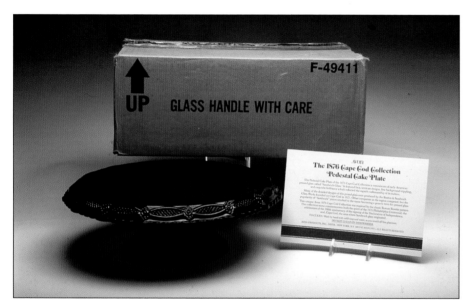

Cake plate with brown shipping box and original brochure.

Pedestal cake plate, 3.5" tall, 10.75" wide, 1991, **$39.00.** Add $1.00 for having the original box. Original selling price $38.00.

# Candle Holders

**Hurricane Candleholder, 10.75" tall**

The special hurricane chimney is 6.75" tall. At the widest part, it is 3.8" wide and at the narrowest part is 2.4" wide. The hurricane candleholder was given the job number AP-72. It was approved for production on March 28, 1985. There were 27 moulds made of the base. Wheaton only made the red base; the clear chimney was contracted out to another company.

We have not discovered who made this unique chimney. It was a special size and shape made to fit the red base. This particular chimney is hard to find on the secondary market if the original gets broke. A standard kerosene chimney will fit into the base but will detract from the original value. The wrong chimney, while workable on the piece, will cause the hurricane to be worth only a third of the value of a correctly matched set.

The chimney flares at the top and has a .5" inset at the base that allows it to sit inside the red base. There are three raised rays on which the chimney sits, to allow the air to circulate when the candle is burning. On the top and bottom of the chimney is a safety lip. It is important that the hurricane has the original chimney to retain its value. These chimneys are extremely hard to find. Care should be taken to keep the wick of the candle trimmed to prevent the chimney from cracking. Another precaution when burning a candle is to put a small amount of water in the base to prevent any extreme heat from coming in contact with the glass when the candle burns down too low.

The red base is 4.5" tall. It is 3.2" wide at the top and 4.35" wide at the base. The bottom of the chimney tapers to fit into the top of the base. Overall height of the hurricane is 10.75" tall. The hurricane was only made in 1985.

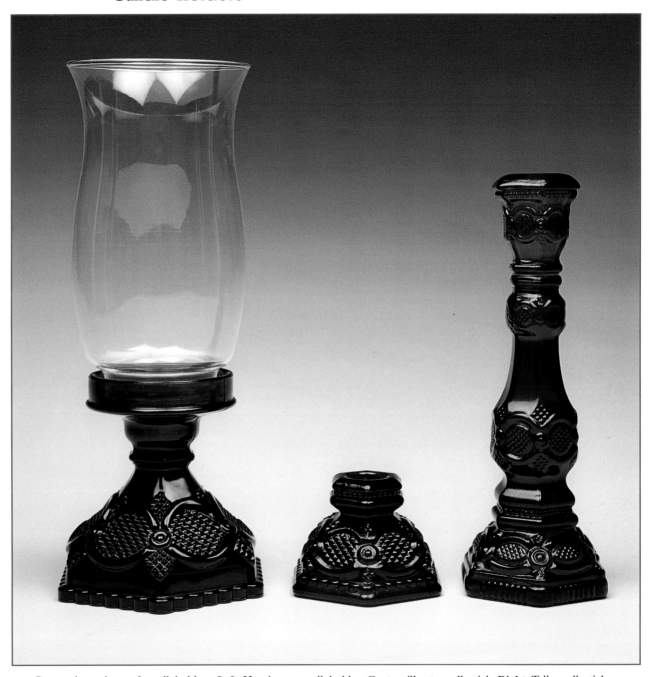

Comparison photo of candleholders. **Left**: Hurricane candleholder, **Center**: Short candlestick, **Right**: Tall candlestick.

35

Hurricane Candle holder shown with shade to the side of the candle holder base. Note: This is the correct shape for the crystal hurricane shade, **$27.50 two-piece set. Base only $7.50. Shade only $14.50. Original selling price $11.00.**

Left: Hurricane candleholder, 10.75" tall, 1985, Right: Original box. Boxed price **$28.50**

## Candlesticks, 2.5" tall

The short candlesticks were approved for production on February 22, 1983. Job number AP-61 was assigned to these. Twenty-five moulds were made for this item.

The candlestick features a hollow base with a six-sided top and bottom. It is 2.5" tall and 3.25" wide. Production was from 1983 to 1984.

Candlestick, 2.5" tall, 1983-1984, $6.00 each

Candlesticks, 2.5" tall, 1983 - 1984, (both with original boxes) **$12.50** pair
**Left:** Candlestick, **Center**: Original box, Right: Candlestick. Original selling
price $18.50 pair

## Candlesticks, 8.75" tall

The tall candlestick is composed of a bottle with a stopper. The job number for the top was S-2755F and the bottom was given the number M-883F. It was approved on April 10, 1975. William Miller designed the bottom on November 7, 1974, drawing number C-21995F. Al Osti designed the top on September 24, 1974, drawing number DE-21994B.

The bottle was filled with Avon's cologne "Charisma." There was an extended line of "Charisma" products. The perfume was to be completely used and the bottle rinsed before burning a candle. A warning was put on the bottom that the contents were flammable, to remind the user to empty the bottle.

The bottle is 6.75" tall and the glass candle top is 2" tall. A clear plastic cork is attached to the base of the stopper to allow it to easily slip into the bottle base. Overall height is 8.75" tall. This candlestick was produced from 1975 to 1980.

Candlesticks, 8.75" tall, 1975-19880, $17.50 pair.
**Left**: Candlestick without top, **Center**: Candlestick top, **Right**: Complete candlestick. These came filled with Charisma cologne. Original selling price $10.00 each

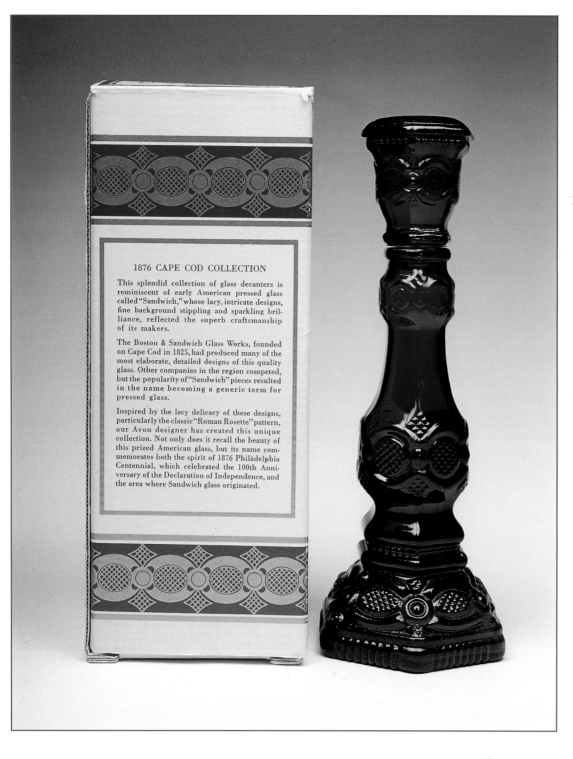

1876 CAPE COD COLLECTION

This splendid collection of glass decanters is reminiscent of early American pressed glass called "Sandwich," whose lacy, intricate designs, fine background stippling and sparkling brilliance, reflected the superb craftsmanship of its makers.

The Boston & Sandwich Glass Works, founded on Cape Cod in 1825, had produced many of the most elaborate, detailed designs of this quality glass. Other companies in the region competed, but the popularity of "Sandwich" pieces resulted in the name becoming a generic term for pressed glass.

Inspired by the lacy delicacy of these designs, particularly the classic "Roman Rosette" pattern, our Avon designer has created this unique collection. Not only does it recall the beauty of this prized American glass, but its name commemorates both the spirit of 1876 Philadelphia Centennial, which celebrated the 100th Anniversary of the Declaration of Independence, and the area where Sandwich glass originated.

**Left:** Original box. **Right**: Tall candlestick, $9.50 boxed price.

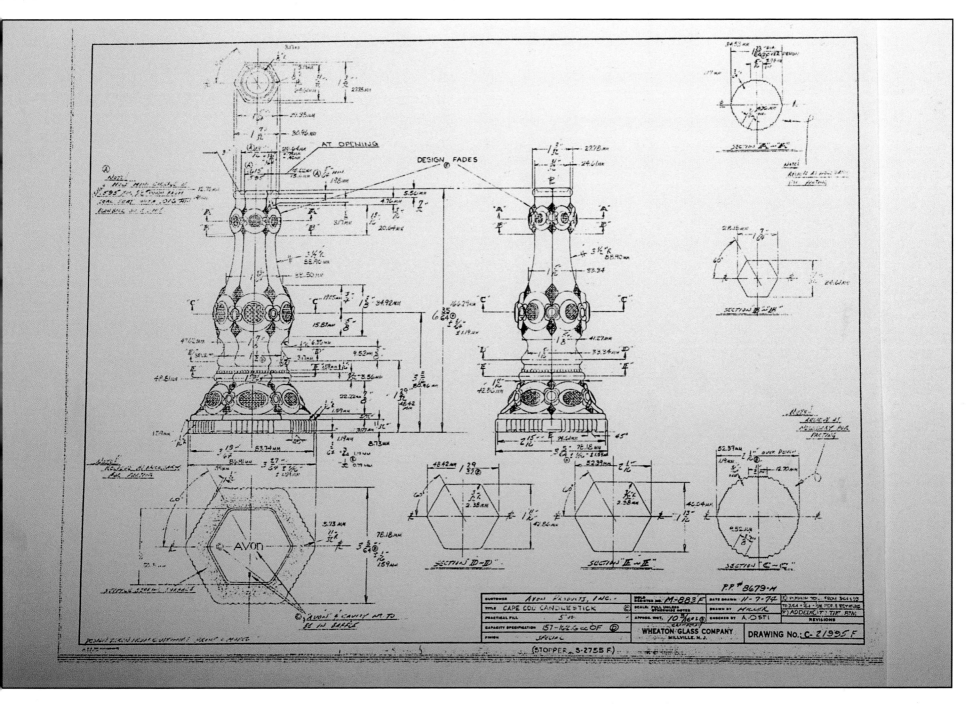

Drawing of candlestick bottom design showing all dimensions and specifications for production. *Reprinted with permission from Wheaton USA.*

Candle cup stopper fits into the candlestick (bottle).

Bottom side of the candlestick showing the Avon paper label listing Charisma cologne, which was the product packaged on the inside.

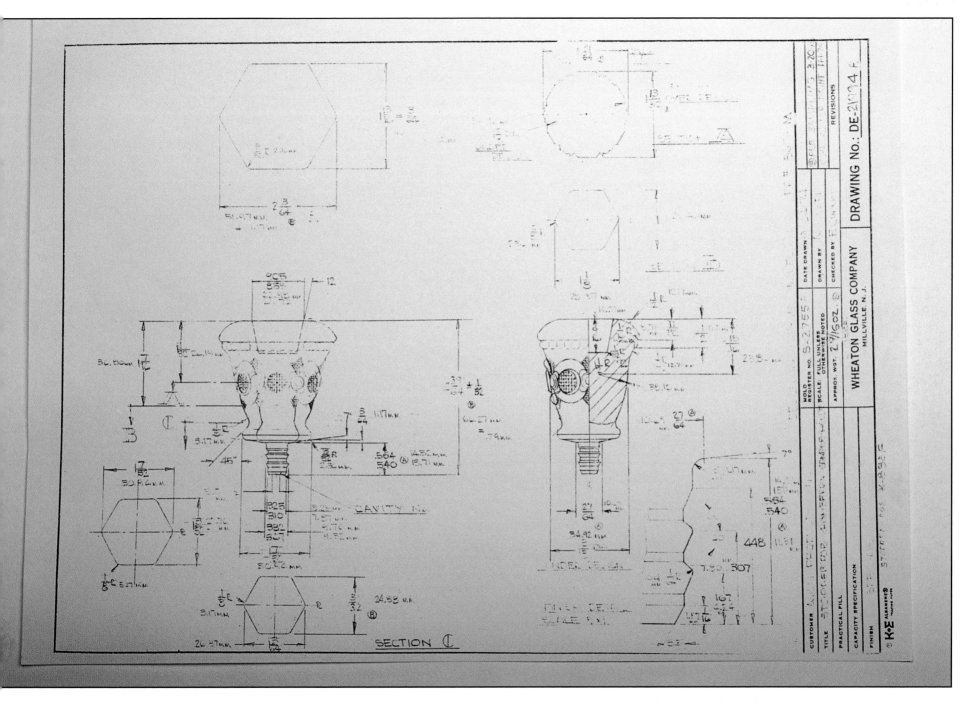

Drawing of candle cup top design showing all dimensions and specifications for production. *Reprinted with permission from Wheaton USA.*

# Candy Dish

**Candy Dish, 6" wide**

    The candy dish was given the job number AP-75 and approved for production on November 13, 1986. There were 24 moulds of this item.

    The footed candy dish has a six-sided base. It is 6" wide and 3.4" tall. Production was from 1987 to 1990. While called a candy dish by Avon, this small footed bowl is a great piece for serving cranberry sauce. This piece can also be used as a small bowl on the table for mayonnaise or a jam.

**Left**: Original box, **Right**: Footed candy dish, 3.4" tall, 6" wide, 1987-1990, Boxed price **$13.50. Original selling price $11.00**

**Opposite page:** Detail of footed candy dish, **$12.50**

# Creamer

**Creamer, 4" tall**

    The footed creamer, job number AP-40, was approved for production on August 7, 1980. Scott Babbitt designed this piece on March 20, 1980. The mould drawing number is C-26692H.

    It holds 5 ounces of liquid and is 4" tall. The creamer was made from 1981 to 1984.

Creamer, 4" tall, 1981-1984, **$6.50. Original selling price $12.00**

**Left**: Original box dated 1990.
**Right**: Creamer. Boxed price **$7.50**

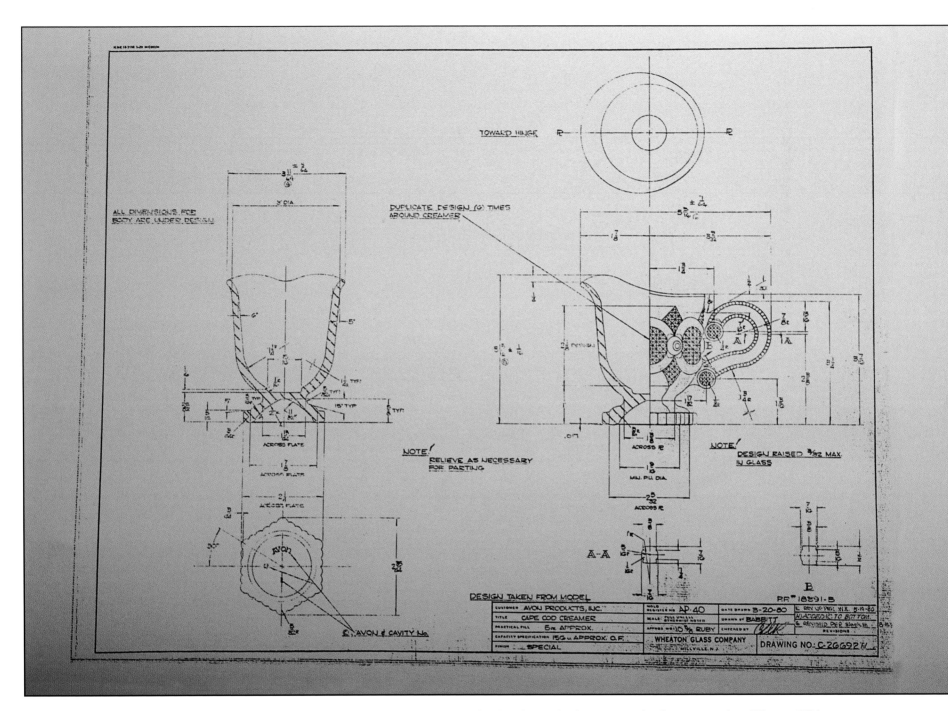

Drawing of creamer design showing all dimensions and specifications for production. *Reprinted with permission from Wheaton USA.*

**Cruet, 8.75" tall**

The cruet, referred to as a pitcher by Wheaton in their production records, had the job number M882F. The stopper was assigned the number S-2753F. Approval was made on April 23, 1975 for production to begin. Al Osti designed this piece on September 26, 1974 on drawing number C-21863G for the base and number E-21864 for the stopper.

"Skin So Soft" bath oil was packaged inside the cruet. There was an extended line of "Skin So Soft" products in the Avon brochures. The bath oil was to be completely used and the cruet cleaned out before using it. A replacement plastic stopper was issued with each cruet so there would be no contamination when it was filled with oil or vinegar for use on the table.

The cruet base is 4.75" tall. The stopper is 2.25" tall. A clear plastic insert is attached to the base of the stopper to allow it to easily slip into the cruet base. Overall height is 5.75" and it holds 5 ounces of liquid. The cruet was made from 1975 to 1980.

Cruet, 5.75" tall, 5 ounces, 1975 - 1980, **$9.50**
Add $1.00 for having the original box.
Original selling price $11.00

1876 Cape Cod Collection
CRUET
SKIN-SO-SOFT BATH OIL
Fill tub. Pour in 1 Teaspoonful. Avoid direct contact with styrene plastics.
KEEP OUT OF REACH OF CHILDREN.
5 FL. OZ.
3 1 0 1
AVON PRODUCTS, INC., NEW YORK, N.Y. 10019

Bottom side of the cruet showing the Avon paper label listing the "Skin So Soft" bath oil that was packaged inside.

Cruet shown with the stopper off to the side.

Detail of cruet stopper.

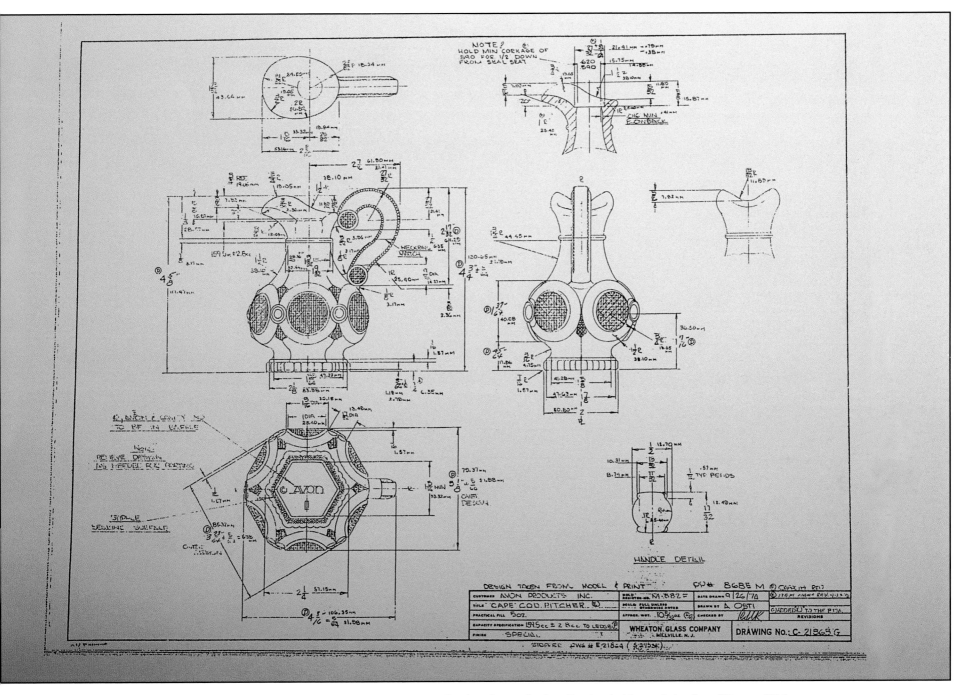

Drawing of cruet design showing all dimensions and specifications for production. *Reprinted with permission from Wheaton USA.*

## Cup and Saucer

The cup, job number AP-83, was approved for production on July 17, 1989. There were 28 moulds made for this item. The saucer, job number AP-82, was approved on June 19, 1989 with 28 moulds being made.

For 1990, in celebration of 1876 Cape Cod Collection being made for 15 years, a special cup was made. The backstamp for this cup read 1975 © AVON [in block letters] 1990. The cup was only marked this way during the 1990 year. The following year, a cup was put into production with the backstamp © AVON [in block letters].

The cup is 3.25" tall and holds 7 ounces of liquid. The saucer is 5.5" wide. The cup and saucer were made from 1990 to 1993, with the special cup only being made in 1990. Numerous collectors have told us that the cup is a perfect size for a votive candle to use as an accent piece on the table.

Cup and saucer, 1990 - 1993, special issue **$13.50**
regular issue **$12.50**
**Left**: Saucer, 5.5" in diameter
**Right**: Coffee cup, 3.25" tall, 7 ounces.
Original selling price $12.00

Cup and saucer, 1990-1993. Coffee cup in the saucer.

Detail of backstamp on bottom of special issue cup, for 1990 only.

Detail of backstamp on bottom of regular issue cup.

**Left**: Original box, **Right**: Cup and saucer.
Add $1.00 for having the original box.

# Decanter

**Decanter, 9.5" tall**

Bill Gibson designed the wine decanter, as Avon referred to it. The bottom part of the decanter appears on mould drawing C-23876H, drawn November 01, 1976. Job number RL-191F was assigned to this. Roy Cramer designed the stopper on mould drawing E-24026D on January 12, 1977. Job number RS-2800F was given to the stopper.

The decanter came filled with bubble bath. The bubble bath was to be completely used and the decanter cleaned out before using it. A replacement plastic stopper was issued with each decanter so there would be no contamination when it was filled with wine for use on the table.

The decanter is 8" tall and holds 16 ounces of liquid. The stopper is 2.5" tall. A red plastic insert screws onto the base of the stopper to allow it to easily slip into the decanter base. This is the only piece to have a matching red plastic insert. Overall height is 9.5" tall. The decanter was made from 1977 to 1980.

Wine decanter, 9.5" tall, 1977-1980, **$12.50**
Add $1.00 for having the original box.
Original selling price $20.00

55

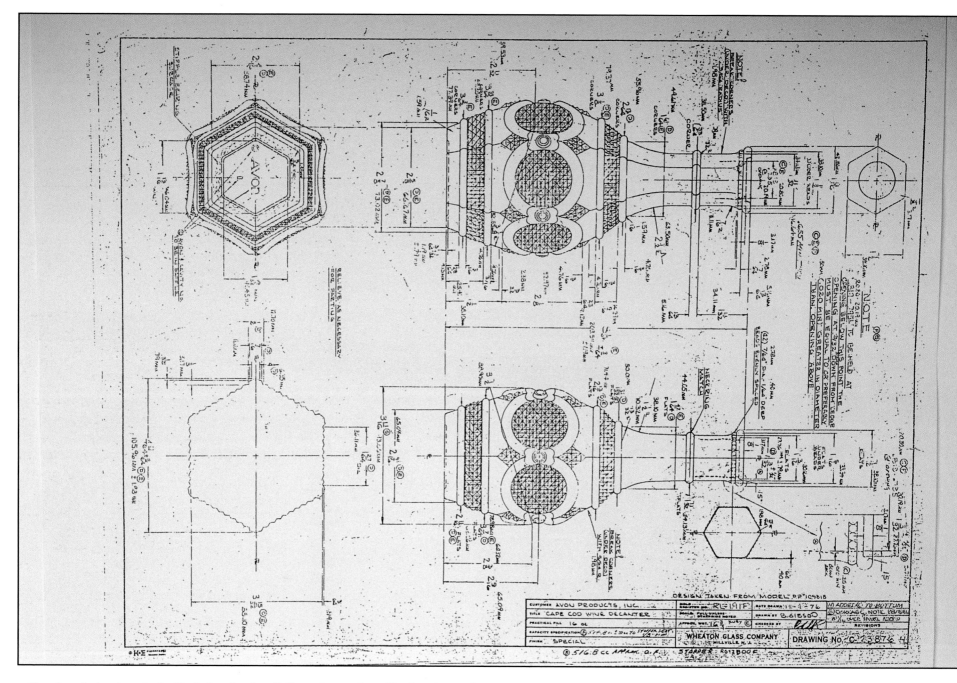

Drawing of wine decanter bottle design showing all dimensions and specifications for production. *Reprinted with permission from Wheaton USA.*

Wine decanter with stopper shown off to the side of the decanter.

Detail of decanter stopper with plastic insert unscrewed from the glass part.

Lamp made from a decanter. We have seen these in the market place and people have frequently asked where they come from. This lamp si not an original item from Avon, but was made by an individual. It is pictured here to show what can be made from such a piece. The price is for its usefulness or decorative look and would not have any collector value. The price for the complete lamp is $24.50.

AVON 1876 CAPE COD COLLECTION
WINE DECANTER
Bubble Bath
TO USE:
POUR 1 TABLESPOONFUL
UNDER RUNNING WATER.
16 FL. OZ.
42987
AVON PRODUCTS, INC., NEW YORK, N.Y. 10019

Bottom side of the decanter showing the Avon paper label listing the bubble bath that was packaged inside.

57

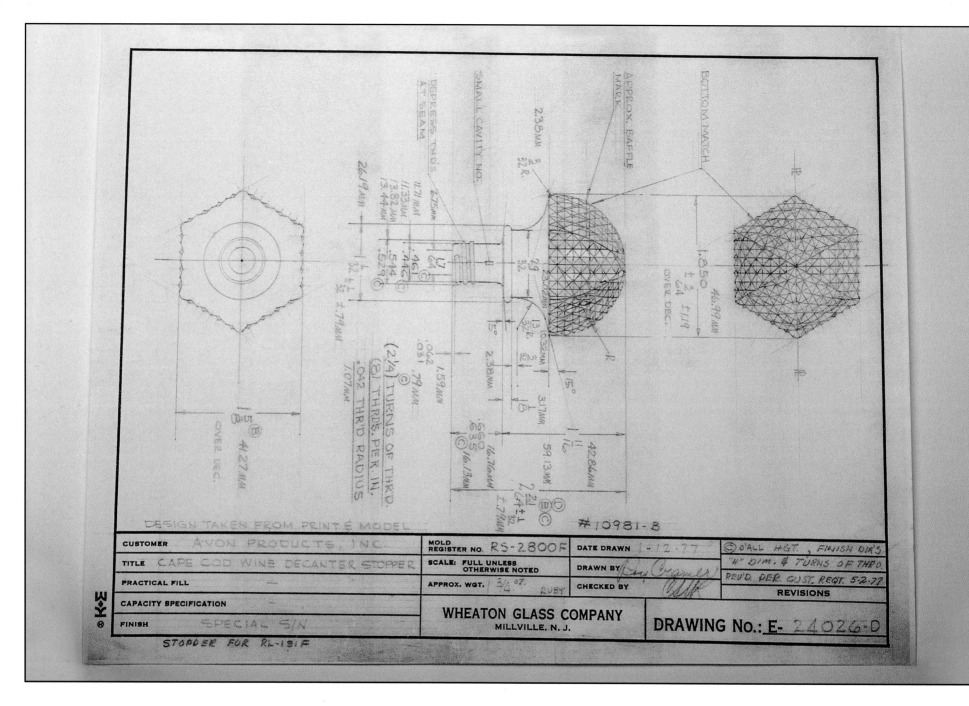

Drawing of wine decanter stopper design showing all dimensions and specifications for production. *Reprinted with permission from Wheaton USA.*

**Dessert Server, 9.5" long**

The dessert server, as Avon referred to it or cake knife by collectors, was initially to be made of glass. The original design of this pattern called for the handle to be made of red glass. The Regent Sheffield Company of England made the metal blade. Unforeseen problems developed with the metal blade not attaching to the glass properly. After several unsuccessful attempts, the knife was sent to the Wheaton plastics division to have the handle made in a matching red plastic. This is the only major item in the collection to be made with a plastic.

The metal blade is extremely sharp stainless steel. Care should be taken when using and cleaning this knife. The blade is 5.5" long and 2" wide. The red plastic handle is 4" long. The total length is 9.5". The dessert server was made from 1981 to 1984.

Dessert server (cake knife), 9.5" long, 2" wide, 1981-1984, **$11.50** Original selling price $12.50.

**Top**: Original box, **Bottom**: Dessert server (cake knife), Boxed price **$12.50**

Detail of marks found on the blade of the dessert server (cake knife).

60

# Goblets

**Wine Goblet, 4.5" tall**

The wine goblet, or goblet "candlette" as Avon referred to it, was designed by Roy Cramer. The Wheaton mould drawing number DE-22966 shows that it was drawn on December 08, 1975. The job number assigned to the wine was AP-27 and was approved for production on March 19, 1976. There were 28 moulds made for this item. The goblet came with a candle that was set into the bowl. It made a nice soft glowing light when lighted.

Comparison photo of stemware sizes.
**Left to right**: Wine goblet, elegant wine (claret), saucer champagne, water goblet.

Wine goblet, 4.5" tall, 3 ounces, 1976-1980, regular issue $2.50; special issue $3.00. Add $0.50 for having the original box. Original selling price $8.00.

## THE 1876 CAPE COD COLLECTION

This splendid goblet is reminiscent of early American pressed glass called "Sandwich Glass." It featured lacy, intricate designs, fine background stippling and exquisite brilliance, which reflected the superb craftsmanship of its makers.

Many of the detailed designs of this prized glass were produced by the Boston & Sandwich Glass Works, founded on Cape Cod in 1825. Other companies in the region competed, but the popularity of "Sandwich" pieces resulted in the name becoming a generic term for pressed glass.

Inspired by the lacy delicacy of these designs, particularly the classic "Roman Rosette" pattern, Avon has created this unique collection. Not only does it recall the beauty of this quality glass, but its name commemorates both the spirit of the 1876 Philadelphia Centennial, which celebrated the 100th Anniversary of the Declaration of Independence, and the area where Sandwich glass originated.

PULL APART HERE. ▶
PUSH DOWN ON METAL DISC TO RELEASE CANDLETTE.

## AVON
# BAYBERRY
### FRAGRANCE CANDLETTE REFILL
### HEIGHT: 1½ IN.

This Avon Fragrance Candlette Refill is molded with a special material that snuffs out the candlette at the end of its burning. The colored residue left at the bottom is this material. For proper and cautious burning, use only Avon Refills with Avon Candle Holders. Clean Holder thoroughly before refilling.

Important Burning Instructions:
- Place Avon Candlette in holder before lighting
- Remove char and trim wick before each use.
- Do not drop burned matches or foreign objects into candlette. • Keep candlette out of direct drafts.
- Never leave burning candlette unattended.

AVON PRODUCTS, INC., DISTR.
NEW YORK, N.Y. 10019    A00542
Printed in U.S.A.

Detail of candle packaged with wine goblet.

Detail of backstamp on the original wine goblet.

**Left**: Original box, **Center**: Perfumed candle that was packaged with goblet, **Right**: Wine goblet. Add $1.00 for having the original candle.

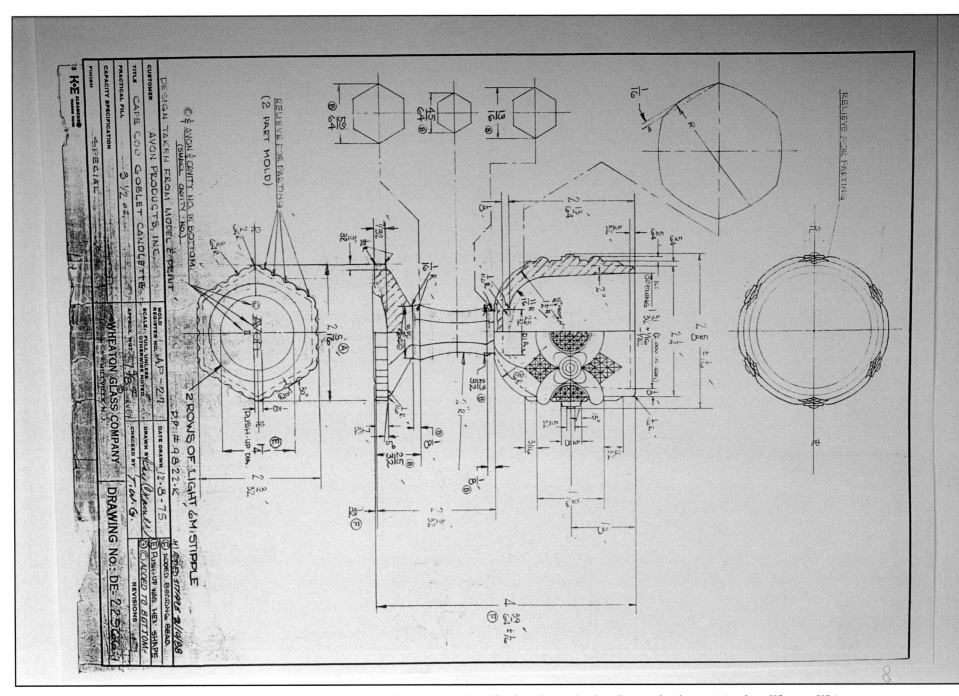

Drawing of original wine goblet design showing all dimensions and specifications for production. *Reprinted with permission from Wheaton USA.*

Another mould drawing, number DE-23246B, shows that the original wine bottom read "© AVON," but it was changed to read "Avon President's Celebration 1976" on July 31, 1976. The job number was changed to AP-27L and was approved for production on March 31, 1976. The special wine was only available for the first year.

The hexagonal shaped foot and stem on the wine match the six ovals in the pattern on the round bowl. The overall height is 4.5" tall and it holds 3 ounces of liquid. This wine was in production from 1976 to 1980.

Detail of backstmp on special-issue wine goblet.

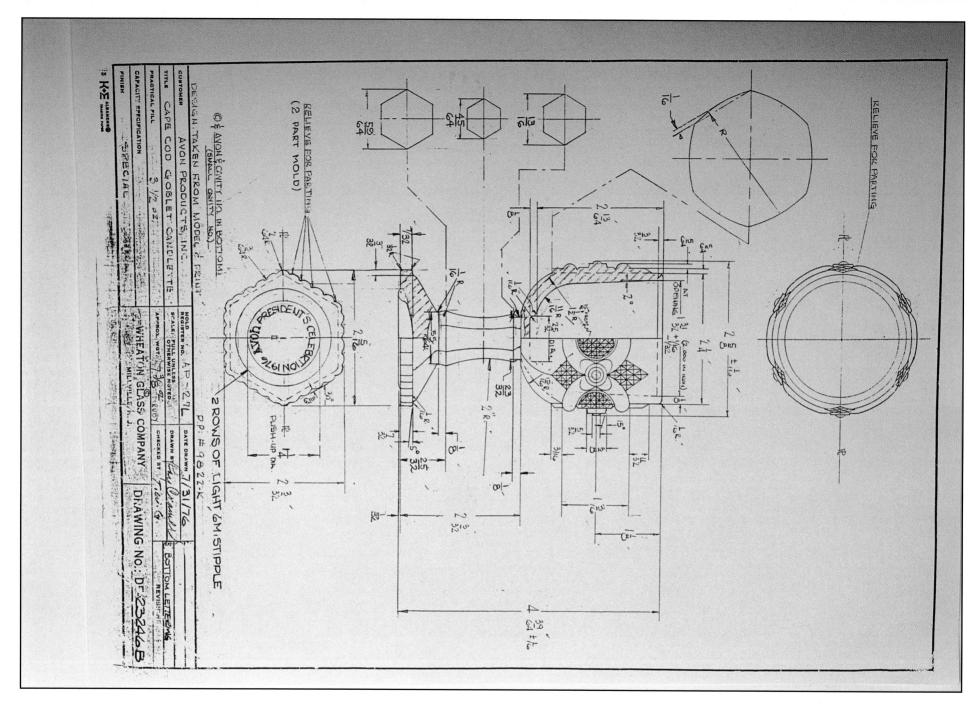

Drawing of special edition wine goblet design showing all dimensions and specifications for production.
Marked - "Avon Presidents Celebration 1976". *Reprinted with permission from Wheaton USA.*

## Elegant Wine Goblet (Claret), 5.25" tall

The elegant wine, as Avon referred to it, or claret goblet, was assigned job number AP-90. It was approved for production on July 29, 1991. There were 26 moulds of this item.

Like the other wine, this one also had a hexagonal shaped foot and stem. These match the six ovals in the pattern on the round bowl. Two goblets came boxed together.

The claret is 5.25" tall and holds 5 ounces of liquid. Production was only made in 1992. This short period of production time makes this another hard-to-find item.

Elegant wine (Claret) with original box.

Elegant wine (Claret), 5.25" tall, 5 ounces, 1992 only, **$9.50**
Add $1.00 for having the original box.
Original selling price $7.00

## Saucer Champagne Goblet, 5.4" tall

The saucer champagne goblet was assigned job number AP-87. It was approved for production on February 25, 1991. There were 24 moulds of this item.

The hexagonal shaped foot and stem on the champagne match the six ovals in the pattern on the round bowl. Two goblets came boxed together.

The champagne is 5.4" tall and holds 8 ounces of liquid. Production was only made in 1991. This short production time makes this another hard-to-find item.

Saucer champagne, 5.4" tall, 8 ounces, 1991 only, **$8.50**

**Left**: Saucer champagne, **Center**: Original box, **Right**: Saucer champagne, Boxed set (2 per box) **$18.00. Original selling price $14.00.**

## Water Goblet, 5.8" tall

The water goblet was designed by Bill Gibson. Mould drawing number D-23631K shows that it was drawn on September 21, 1976. It was assigned job number AP-28 and was approved for production on December 28, 1976. There were 26 moulds of this item. This goblet came boxed with a perfumed candle.

Like the other three goblets, the water goblet also had a hexagonal shaped foot and stem that match the six ovals in the pattern on the round bowl. The water goblet is 5.8" tall and holds 9 ounces of liquid. This water goblet was in production from 1977 to 1990.

Water goblet.
Add $1.00 for having the original candle.

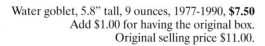

Water goblet, 5.8" tall, 9 ounces, 1977-1990, **$7.50**
Add $1.00 for having the original box.
Original selling price $11.00.

70

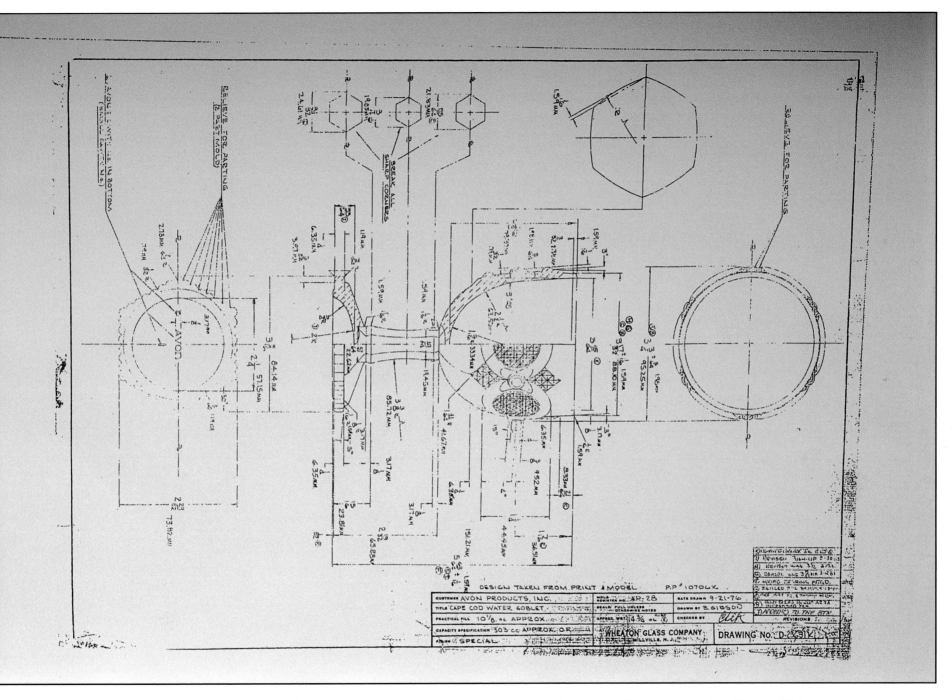

Drawing of water goblet design showing all dimensions and specifications for production. *Reprinted with permission from Wheaton USA.*

# Gravy Boat

**Gravy Boat, 8" long**

    The gravy boat, or footed sauce boat as Avon referred to it, was given the job number AP-79. It was approved for production on March 13, 1988. The oblong hexagonal footed sauce boat has three oval designs on each side. Most collectors call this a gravy boat. There were 24 moulds of this item.

    Overall length is 8" long, 3.4" wide, and 4" tall. Production was only made in 1988. It is a hard-to-find item.

**Gravy** (footed sauce) boat, 3.75" tall, 8" long, 1988 only, **$19.50. Original selling price $14.00.**

**Top**: Gravy (footed sauce) boat, **Bottom**: Original box, Boxed price $20.50

## THE 1876 CAPE COD COLLECTION

The footed sauce boat of the 1876 Cape Cod Collection is reminiscent of early American pressed glass called "Sandwich Glass." It featured lacy, intricate designs, fine background stippling, and exquisite brilliance which reflected the superb craftsmanship of its makers.

Many of the detailed designs of this prized glass were produced by the Boston & Sandwich Glass Works founded on Cape Cod in 1825. Other companies in the region competed, but the popularity of "Sandwich" pieces resulted in the name becoming a generic term for pressed glass.

This unique Avon 1876 Cape Cod Collection was inspired by the classic Roman Rosette pattern. The collection name commemorates both the spirit of the 1876 Philadelphia Centennial, the celebration of the 100th anniversary of the signing of the Declaration of Independence, and, Cape Cod, the area where Sandwich glass orignated.

AVON PRODUCTS, INC., DISTR., NEW YORK, N.Y. 10019
© AVON 1988—ALL RIGHTS RESERVED

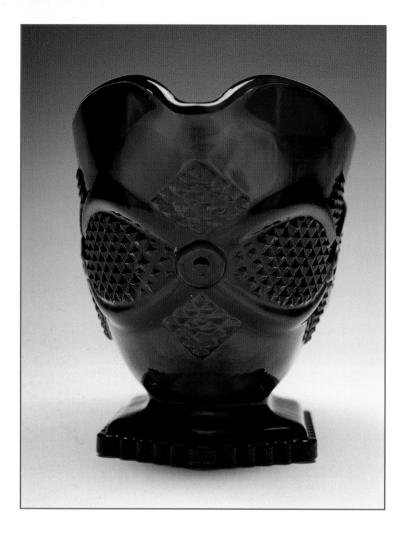

Front view of gravy (footed sauce) boat.

Top view of gravy (footed sauce) boat.

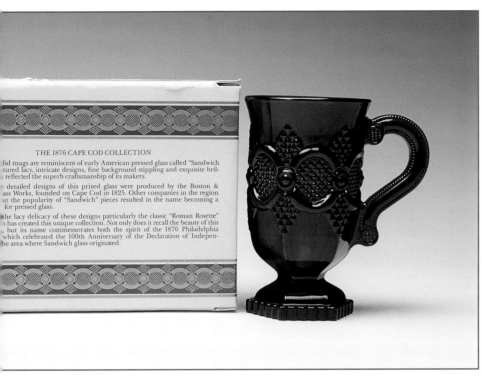

THE 1876 CAPE COD COLLECTION

...did mugs are reminiscent of early American pressed glass called "Sandwich ...tured lacy, intricate designs, fine background stippling and exquisite bril... ...reflected the superb craftsmanship of its makers.

...detailed designs of this prized glass were produced by the Boston & ...ass Works, founded on Cape Cod in 1825. Other companies in the region ...ut the popularity of "Sandwich" pieces resulted in the name becoming a ...for pressed glass.

...the lacy delicacy of these designs particularly the classic "Roman Rosette" ...n has created this unique collection. Not only does it recall the beauty of this ...but its name commemorates both the spirit of the 1876 Philadelphia ...which celebrated the 100th Anniversary of the Declaration of Indepen- ...he area where Sandwich glass originated.

Pedestal mug, 5" tall, 6 ounces, 1982-1984, Boxed set (2 per box) **$16.00**
**Left:** Mug, **Center:** Original box, **Right:** Mug. Original selling price $17.50 pair.

## Pedestal Mug, 5" tall

The pedestal mug, as Avon referred to it, was designed by William Miller. Mould drawing number C-27988A shows that it was done on May 26, 1982. It was assigned job number AP-49 by Wheaton and was approved for production on December 02, 1981. There were 29 moulds of this item.

The hexagonal shaped foot matches the six ovals in the pattern on the round bowl. The beaded S-shaped handle sets it off nicely. The mug is 5" tall and holds 6 ounces of liquid. This mug was in production from 1982 to 1984.

Pedestal mug, 5" tall, 6 ounces, 1982-1984, **$7.50**

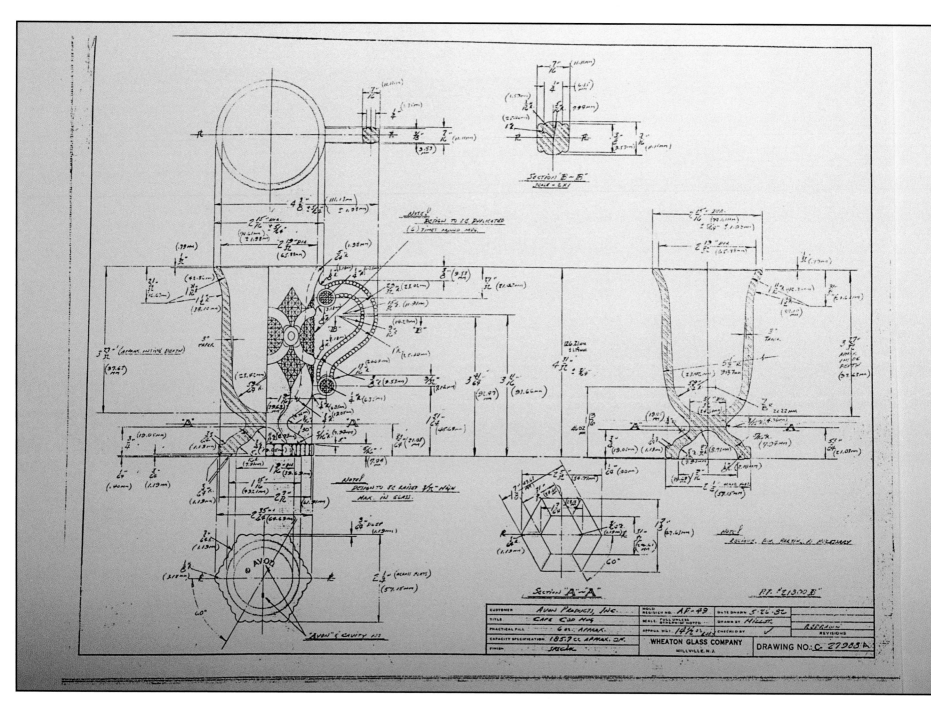

Drawing of pedestal mug design showing all dimensions and specifications for production. *Reprinted with permission from Wheaton USA.*

## Napkin Ring Holder, 1.75" wide

The napkin ring holders were assigned job number S-3718F. Ed Magee designed the mould in drawing number E-32697C on March 15, 1988. Design was approved for production on February 02, 1989. Inside one end is a beveled edge. It is slightly rough where it came out of the mould and had to be ground out. The other side has a smooth edge. They were packaged four to a boxed set.

The holders are 1.75" in diameter and 1.3" tall. Production was from 1989 to 1990.

Detail of napkin rings, **$7.50** each

Napkin rings, 1.75" wide, 1989-1990, Boxed set (4 per box) **$31.00**
**Back**: Original box, **Front**: Set of four napkin rings. Original selling price $12.00

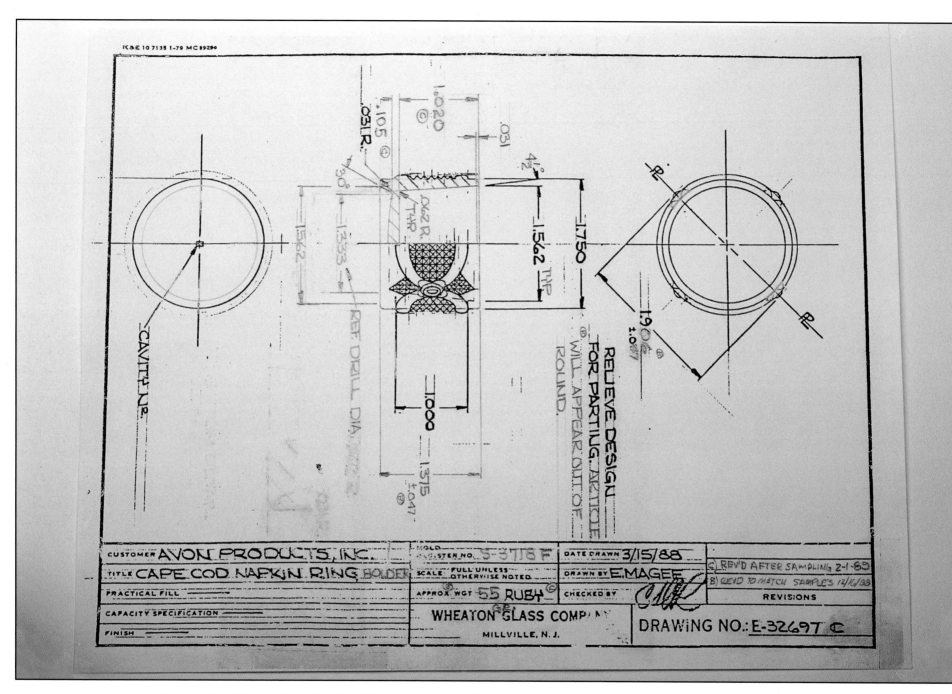

Drawing of napkin ring design showing all dimensions and specifications for production. *Reprinted with permission from Wheaton USA.*

**Christmas Ornament, 3.25" wide**

The Christmas ornament was approved for production on May 7, 1990. It was given the job number AP-85. For this item there were 27 moulds made.

On one side of the ornament is the typical 1876 Cape Cod pattern. On the other is a flat surface that is recessed. In this area, printed in gold, is the decoration of a sprig of holly with the words "Christmas 1990 ©AVON".

This was the only non-dinnerware item to come with this set. The ornament was usually overlooked when purchasing 1876 Cape Cod and is a hard-to-find item. Being made of solid glass, the ornament hangs too heavy on a real tree, weighing down the branch. The ornament is best suited for hanging on an artificial tree.

The ornament is 2.75" wide and .25" thick. Originally the ornament came with a cloth red and green striped ribbon attached to it. This ribbon is frequently missing and decreases the value of the ornament by $2. On the top is a molded hole for hanging the ornament by a hook or a ribbon. This was offered in 1990 only.

Ornament, 3.25" in diameter, made in 1990 only, **$12.50**
The front side of the ornament is flat and decorated with gold letters reading "Christmas 1990 Avon." Add $1.00 for having the original box. Original selling price $8.00.

Back side of the ornament that has the 1876 Cape Cod pattern.

Ornament with original green and red cloth bow, and with original box.

**Pie Plate Server, 10.75" wide**

The pie plate server, as Avon referred to it, job number AP-91, was approved for production on January 7, 1992. At first glance, the name would seem to suggest this was made to be put in the oven. This is definitely not the case. The glass is not heat resistant and cannot be used in the oven. There must have been some concern over the name, since it was molded on the back, "NOT FOR OVEN USE" in block letters. The idea was to slip the baked pie out of its baking pan and put it in the pie server for decorative table use. A no-bake refrigerator pie is a perfect use for this pie server.

This resembles a larger version of the rim soup. It has a 1.25" flat border on the edge, is 10.75" wide, and 1.5" tall. The pie plate server was one of the last two items designed in the 1876 Cape Cod Collection. Production was from 1992 to 1993.

Pie plate server, 10.75", 1992-1993, **$23.50. Original selling price, $18.00.**

Pie plate server. **Back:** Shown in upright position.
**Front:** Shown flat.

**Left**: Original pie plate server box, **Right**: Pie plate server shown in upright position, Boxed price **$24.50**

Detail of backstamp on pie plate server reading "**NOT FOR OVEN USE**"[ in block letters].

**Water Pitcher, 8.4" tall**

The water pitcher was approved for production on February 2, 1984 with 17 moulds being made. The job number on this item was AP-63. It has a hexagonal shaped footed base and straight sides. There are eight ovals around the center of the pitcher. The pitcher has a molded spout with no ice lip. This is the heaviest of the 1876 Cape Cod pieces, weighing 3.5 pounds. It becomes quite heavy when filled with a liquid.

The pitcher is 8.4" tall to the top of the spout and holds 60 ounces. It was made from 1984 to 1985.

Water pitcher, 8.4" tall, 60 ounces, 1984 1985, **$34.50**
Add $1.00 for having the original box.
Original selling price $20.00.

Note: No ice lip on water pitcher.

Comparison photo of plate sizes. **Left**: Bread and butter, **Center**: Dinner, **Right**: Dessert.

## Bread and Butter Plate, 5.5" wide

The bread and butter plate was given the job number AP-82P. It was approved for production on January 7, 1992. There were 28 moulds that were modified. This was one of the last two items made in the 1876 Cape Cod pattern. This plate was adapted from the saucer by removing the indented ring for holding the cup. These plates were packed two to a box.

The plate is 5.5" wide and was made from 1992 to 1993. This plate is hard to find. Many collectors are missing this plate from their sets.

Bread and butter plate, 5.5" diameter, 1992-1993, $9.50. Add $1.00 for having the original box. Original selling price $6.00.

## Dessert Plate, 7.5" wide

The dessert plate was given the job number AP-34 and was designed by Bud Norcross on January 5, 1979. The drawing number was D-25637D. It was approved on August 22, 1979 for production. There were 28 moulds made. The plates were packed two to a box.

The plate is 7.5" wide and was made from 1980 to 1990.

---

**Back**: Original box, **Front**: Dessert plate, Boxed set (2 per box) **$14.00**
**Original selling price $14.50 pair.**

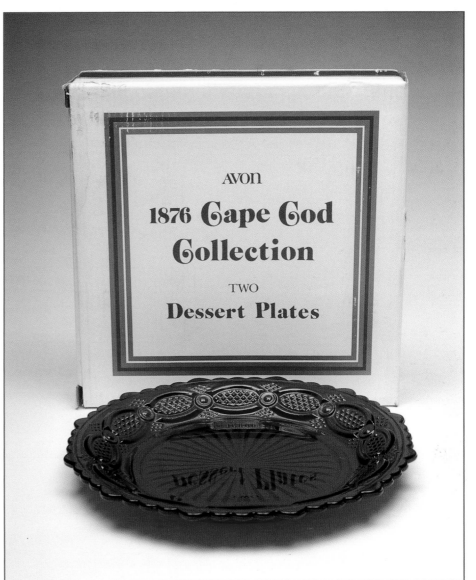

Dessert plate, 7.5" in diameter, 1980-1990, **$6.50**

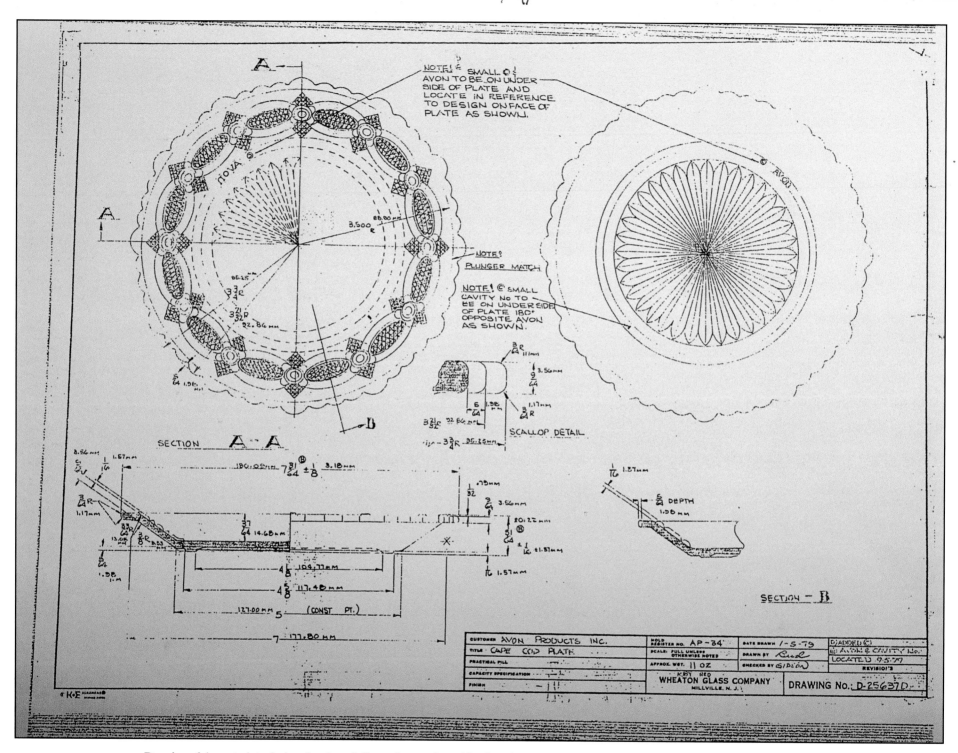

Drawing of dessert plate design showing all dimensions and specifications for production. *Reprinted with permission from Wheaton USA.*

## Dinner Plate, 11" wide

Bill Gibson designed the dinner plate on February 12, 1981. The job number was AP-48 and the drawing number was C-27744C. The dinner plate was approved for production on August 27, 1981 with 19 moulds being made.

The dinner plate is 11" wide and was made from 1982 to 1990.

Back: Original box, Front: Dinner plate, Boxed price **$20.50**

Dinner plate, 11" in diameter, 1982-1990, **$19.50. Original selling price $16.00.**

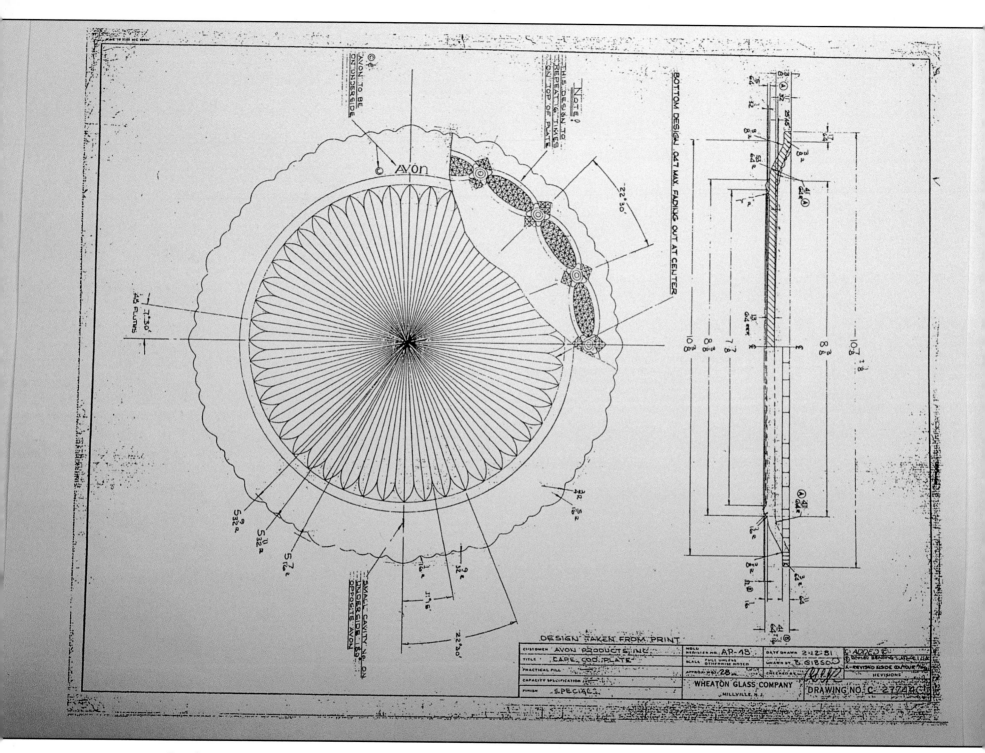

Drawing of dinner plate design showing all dimensions and specifications for production. *Reprinted with permission from Wheaton USA.*

# Platter

**Serving Platter, 13" long**

Job number AP-74, indicates this was the oval serving platter. Approval for production was given on March 24, 1986. Twenty-six moulds were made for this item.

The platter is 13" long and 10.75" wide. Production was only in 1986. This is another one of the accessory items that is hard to find due to its short production time.

The platter is a nice size that can be used for a variety of meats including a beef or pork roast, sliced ham, stuffed chicken or Cornish game hens. The size is even large enough to accommodate a small turkey.

Serving platter, 13" long, 10.75" wide, 1986 only, $45.00. Original selling price $24.00.

**Left**: Original box, **Right**: Serving platter, Boxed price **$46.00**

Back side of serving platter showing that it has a rayed bottom.

## Relish Dish, 9.3" long

The condiment dish, as Avon referred to it, is called a two-part relish by collectors and has the job number AP-70. The mould was approved for production on December 27, 1984. There were 28 moulds made.

The relish is 9.3" long, 5.4" wide, and 1.25" deep. It has a solid divider in the center to make two equal square sections. Production was from 1985 to 1986.

Back: Upright view of divided relish (condiment dish). **Front:** Flat view of relish, price for one **$11.50. Original selling price $12.00.**

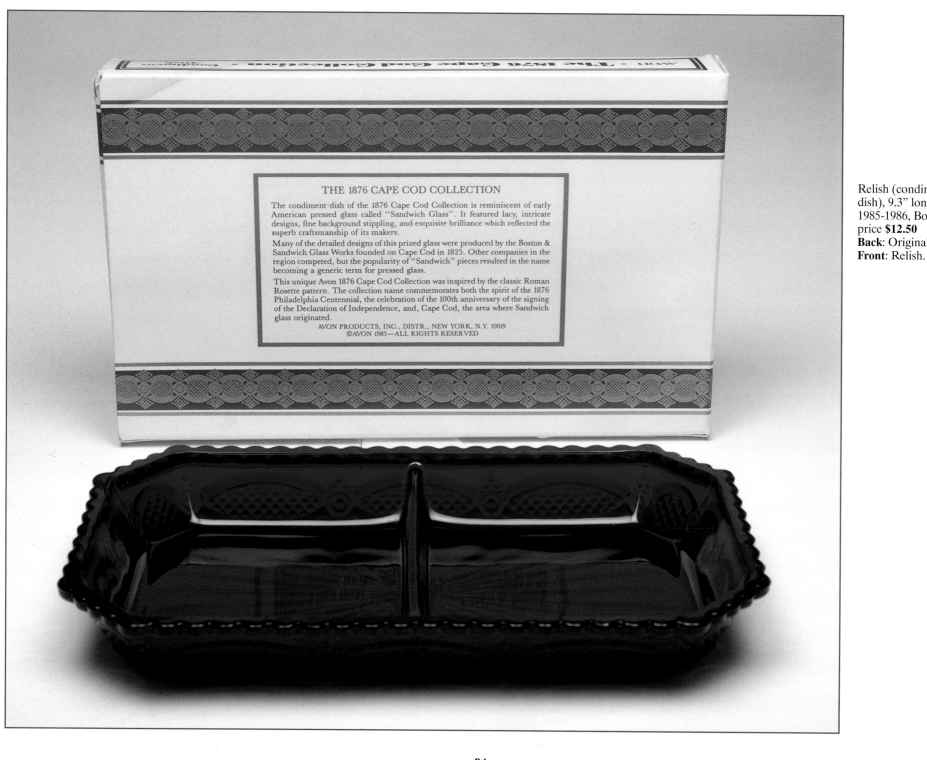

THE 1876 CAPE COD COLLECTION

The condiment dish of the 1876 Cape Cod Collection is reminiscent of early American pressed glass called "Sandwich Glass". It featured lacy, intricate designs, fine background stippling, and exquisite brilliance which reflected the superb craftsmanship of its makers.

Many of the detailed designs of this prized glass were produced by the Boston & Sandwich Glass Works founded on Cape Cod in 1825. Other companies in the region competed, but the popularity of "Sandwich" pieces resulted in the name becoming a generic term for pressed glass.

This unique Avon 1876 Cape Cod Collection was inspired by the classic Roman Rosette pattern. The collection name commemorates both the spirit of the 1876 Philadelphia Centennial, the celebration of the 100th anniversary of the signing of the Declaration of Independence, and, Cape Cod, the area where Sandwich glass originated.

AVON PRODUCTS, INC., DISTR., NEW YORK, N.Y. 10019
©AVON 1985—ALL RIGHTS RESERVED

Relish (condiment dish), 9.3" long, 1985-1986, Boxed price **$12.50**
**Back**: Original box, **Front**: Relish.

# Shakers

## Salt and Pepper Shakers, 4.5" tall

The salt and pepper shakers were given the job number S-2931R. Roy Cramer designed the shakers on June 28, 1977 and they were approved on September 22, 1977. The drawing was given the number DE-24283E. There were 27 moulds made. In celebration of Mother's Day 1978. The bottom of the shakers were marked "AVON May 1978".

Bruce Pierce modified the original mould drawing to eliminate the special mark on April 12, 1978 and it was approved the same day. The new drawing was given the number DE-25247A. The job number changed to S-2931RP. After the Mother's Day offer passed, the shakers were marked on the bottom © AVON [in block letters].

The shakers were filled with the Avon cologne "Topaze." There was an extended line of "Topaze" products in the Avon brochures. The "Topaze" cologne was introduced in 1935 to honor the 50th wedding anniversary of Mr. & Mrs. McConnell, the founders of Avon. The cologne was to be completely used-up and the bottle rinsed before re-using. A warning was put on the bottom that the contents were flammable, to remind the user to empty the shaker. A replacement plastic liner for the shaker top was issued with each shaker, so there would be no contamination when it was filled with salt or pepper for use on the table.

The shakers are 4.5" tall and have matching red plastic lids that screw on. These are the only items with plastic lids. The special shakers were limited to the Spring Campaign of 1978. The other shakers were offered from 1978 to 1980. The shakers with the special marking are very hard to find.

Salt and pepper shakers, 4.5" tall, 1978-1980, regular issue, pair **$12.50**; special issue, pair **$13.50**. Add $1.00 for having the original box. Original selling price $12.00 pair

Salt shaker shown with top off to the side.

Detail of backstamp on special issue shaker, marked "May 1978."

Detail of backstamp on regular shaker.

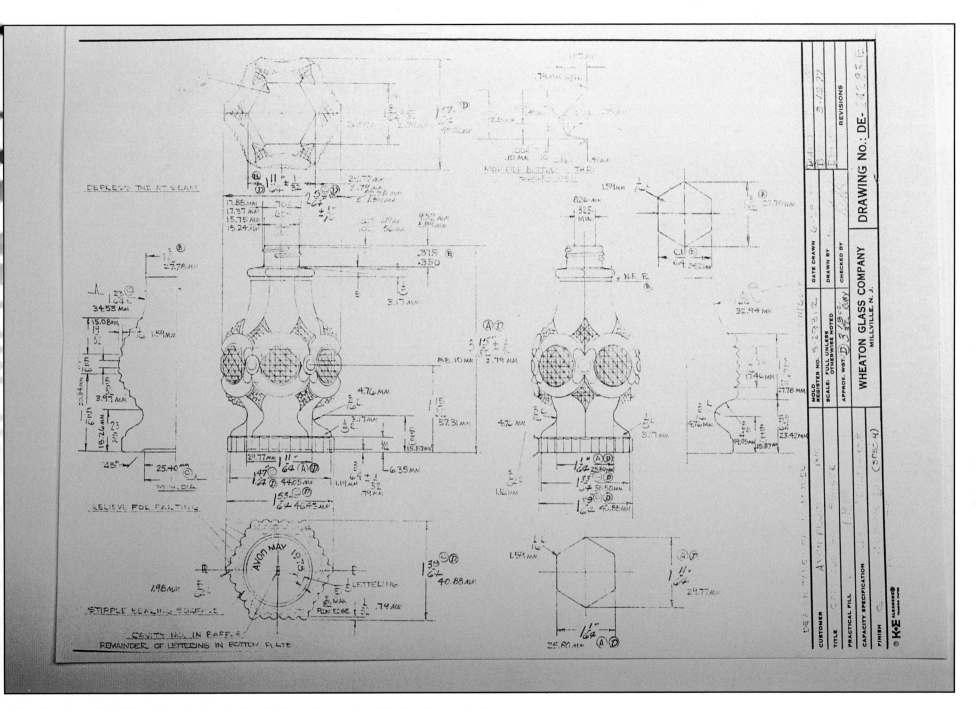

Drawing of special edition shaker design showing all dimensions and specifications for production.
Marked with May 1978. *Reprinted with permission from Wheaton USA.*

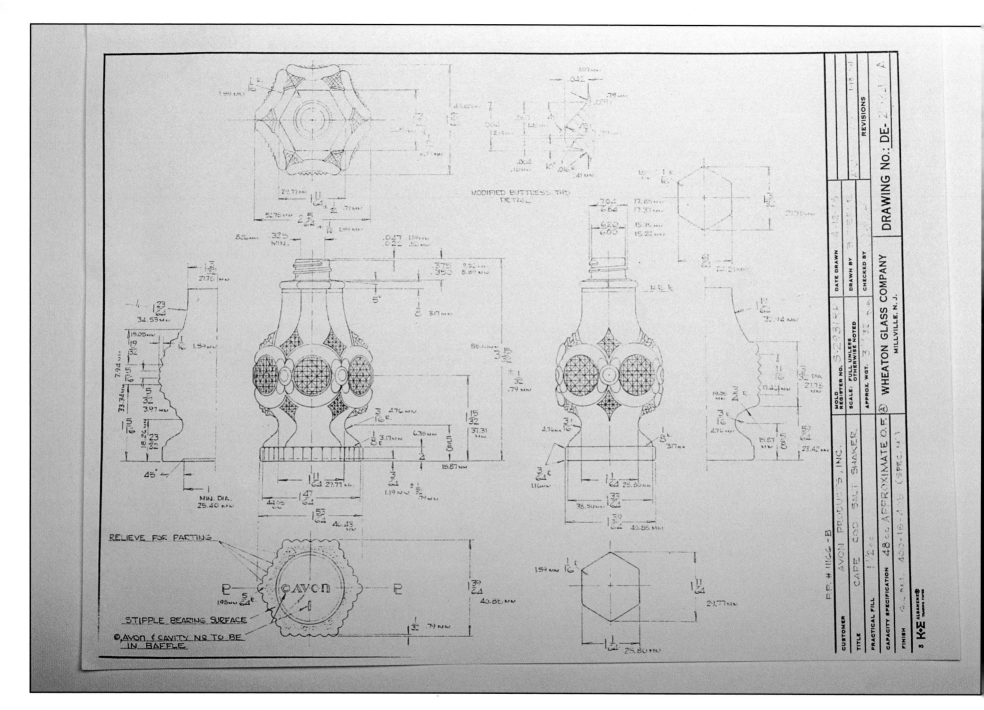

Drawing of regular shaker design showing all dimensions and specifications for production. *Reprinted with permission from Wheaton USA.*

# Sugar Bowl

**Sugar Bowl, 3.35" tall**

The sugar bowl was designed by William Miller on January 18, 1980. The job number is AP-39 and the drawing number is D-26691D. The sugar was approved for production on July 1, 1980. There were 19 moulds made for this item. The sugar was offered from 1980 to 1983 packed with sachet tablets. From 1983 to 1990, the sugar was packed by itself.

The sugar is 3.35" tall and 3.5" wide. It holds 6 ounces. The total length of time the sugar was offered was from 1980 to 1990.

Sugar bowl, 3.35" tall, 1980-1983, $7.50. Original selling price $12.00.

Sugar bowl, 3.5" tall, 1980 - 1983, Boxed price with sachet **$9.50**
**Left**: Original box, **Center**: Sachet, **Right**: Sugar.

1983 - 1990, Boxed price **$8.50**
**Left**: Original box dated 1990, **Right**: Sugar.

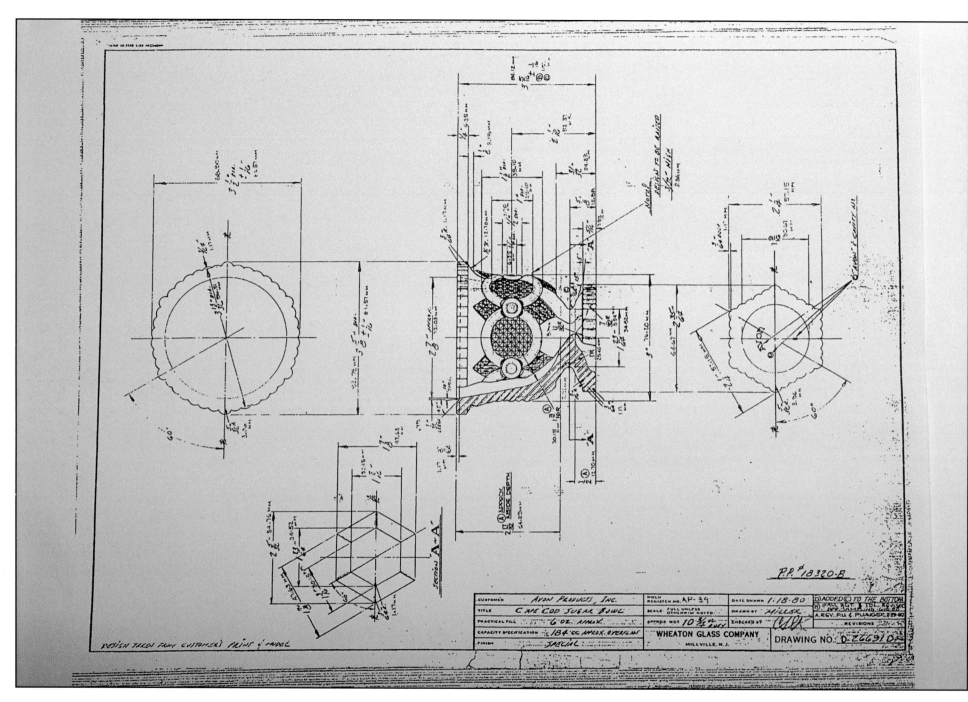

Drawing of sugar bowl design showing all dimensions and specifications for production. *Reprinted with permission from Wheaton USA.*

**Footed Glass,
3.75" tall**

The footed glass, as Avon referred to it, is also known as a high-ball tumbler by collectors. It was given the job number AP-78 and was approved on January 12, 1988. Thirty moulds were made of this item. The tumblers were packaged two to a box.

This is a hexagonal shaped, footed, short tumbler that holds 8 ounces of liquid. It is 3.75" tall. The tumbler was only offered in 1988.

Comparison photo of tumbler sizes.
**Left**: Footed glass (high ball tumbler), **Right**: Tall beverage glass (tumbler).

Footed glass (high ball tumbler), 3.75" tall, 8 ounces,
1988 only, **$7.50**

Footed glass (high ball tumbler), 3.75" tall, 8 ounces,
1988 only, Boxed set (2 per box) **$16.00**
**Back**: Original box, **Front:** Tumblers.
Original selling price $12.00

AVON
The
1876 Cape Cod Collection
Footed Glass Set · Contains 2 Glasses

**Tall Beverage Glass, 5.5" tall**

The tall beverage glass, as Avon referred to it, or tall beverage tumbler, was given the job number AP-84. Approval of the mould was given on January 11, 1990. Twenty-seven moulds were made of this item. The tumblers were packaged two to a box.

This has a hexagonal base and straight sides. It holds 12 ounces of liquid. The tumbler measures 5.5" tall. The tumbler was only offered in 1990.

Tall beverage glass (tumbler), 5.5" tall, 12 ounces, 1990 only, **$9.50**

**Left**: Tall beverage glass (tumbler), **Center**: Original box, **Right**: Tall beverage glass (tumbler). Boxed set (2 per box) **$20.00**.
**Original selling price $14.00.**

# Two-tier Server

**Two-tier Server, 10.25" tall**

The two-tier server is made up of two plates: a dessert plate and a dinner plate, with a metal centerpiece to hold them in a tiered position. Some collectors refer to this piece as a tidbit server. The large plate was modified from the dinner plate mould by designer Bob O'Donnell on February 4, 1987. The new drawing number is C-31489D and the new job number assigned was AP-48T. The plate was changed to have a center hole and an indent on the bottom to fit in the metal handle.

Bob O'Donnell also modified the dessert plate to be the small plate for the two-tier server. The new drawing number for it is D-331490B and the job number was changed to AP-34T. This was done on March 7, 1986, The only change was the addition of the hole in the center. The new plate was made to accommodate the metal center handle.

The metal handle was contracted out to another company to meet Avon's specifications. Overall height is 10.25" tall. The bottom plate is 11" wide and the top plate is 7.5" wide. Approval was given to produce the server on February 24, 1987. The two tier server was offered in 1987 only.

Two-tier Server (tidbit), 10.25" tall, 1987 only, **$45.00**
Add $1.00 for having the original box.
Original selling price $24.00.

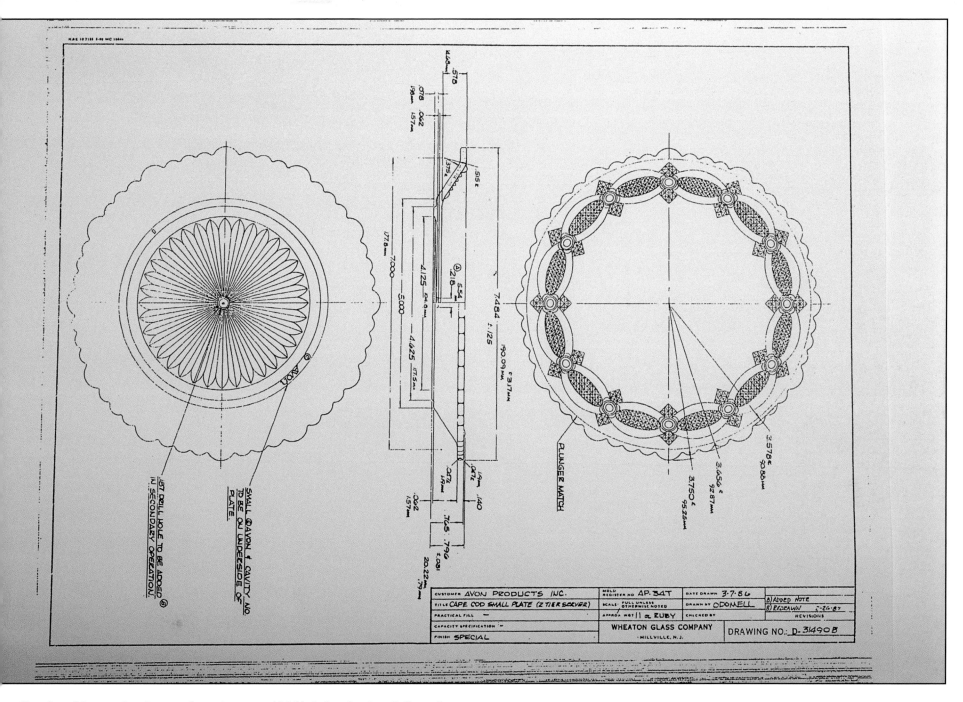

Drawing of dessert plate for top of two-tier server (tidbit) design showing all dimensions and specifications for production. *Reprinted with permission from Wheaton USA.*

Back side of the bottom plate on the two-tier server (tidbit) showing how the dinner plate was adapted for another use.

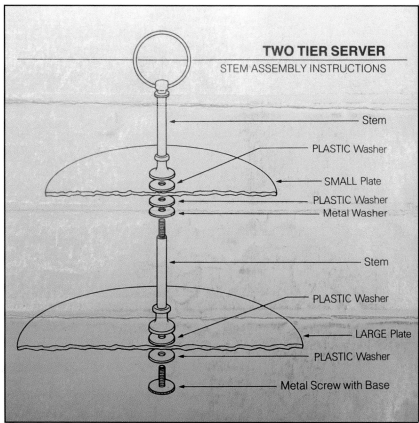

Original 1876 Cape Cod brochure from two-tier server showing how it is to be assembled.

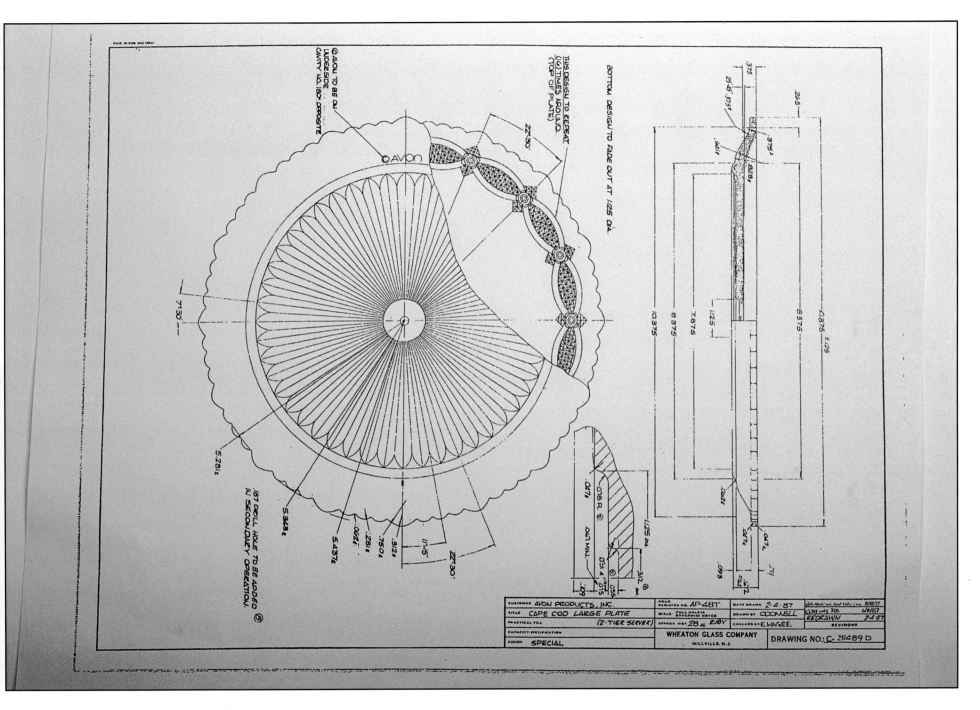

Drawing of dinner plate for bottom of two-tier server design showing all dimensions and specifications for production. Note: Mould was changed to have a center recessed area to accommodate the bottom flat metal bolt. *Reprinted with permission from Wheaton USA.*

Two-tier Server (tidbit) with original box.

Vase, footed, 8" tall, 1985 only, **$13.50**.
Add $1.00 for having the original box.
Original selling price **$12.00**

# Vase

**Vase, 8" tall**

The footed vase was given the job number AP-65 and approved for production on April 27, 1984. There were 22 moulds made for this item.

The hexagonal shaped footed vase has a short two-ring stem and flares to the top. The vase is 8" tall and 4.5" wide across the top. It was produced for one year only, in 1985.

During the last year of production of Cape Cod in 1993, Avon decided to offer matching linens as a finale to the pattern. The Bucilla Corporation, well known for fine needlecrafts, developed the special embroidery kits that were made to match the Avon Cape Cod pattern. Avon offered the kits during one of their campaigns. There are two different packages: #63399 table runner and #63400 eight matching napkins. In the kit was the white polyester cotton blend material that was stamped with the Cape Cod pattern. The permanent press material was machine washable. Also included was the red embroidery floss thread used to sew the different stitches on the stamped design. The instructions show all the different types of stitches in the various areas of the pattern along with the directions on how to do the stitches. After completing all the stitches, the material was to be washed in lukewarm water and allowed to air dry. The finished table runner is 44" long and 13.5" wide. The napkins are each 13.5" square. When finished these items make an attractive accent for your table set with the beautiful red Cape Cod dishes.

Bucilla package of table runner, **$14.50**

Bucilla package of napkins, **$14.50**

Page 1 of the instructions for the kit, including introduction and guidelines.

Page 2 of the instructions for the kit, including the type of stitches to be used.

The plain material showing stamped outlines on where the stitches will go, along with red thread and needle.

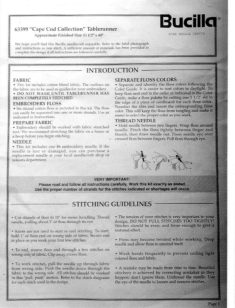

Close-up of embroidery stitches.

# Resources

It is important to know what resources exist to assist you with your collecting. There are various resources listed below to help you obtain information on your particular item.

National Association of Avon Collector's Clubs
Attention: Connie Clark
P.O. Box 7006, Kansas City, Missouri 64113
This resource will help you find a local Avon club or assist you in getting one started in your area.

*Avon Times*
Attention: Vera and Dwight Young
P.O Box 9868, Kansas City, Missouri 64134
816-540-3089
24/year for 8 newsletters
email: avontimes@aol.com

Avon Products, Inc. has a website to provide information about their products. http://shop.avon.com

Wheaton Village
1501 Glasstown Road, Millville, New Jersey
has numerous educational activities and exhibits
Tel: 856-825-6800 or check their web site: www.wheatonvillage.org

# Bibliography

Avon Products, Inc. Company Brochures. New York. 1975 to 1995.

Barlow, Raymond & Joan Kaiser. *The Glass Industry in Sandwich.* West Chester, Pennsylvania: Schiffer Publishing Ltd., 1987.

Chance, Everett. Personal conversations and correspondence. Millville, New Jersey. 2002.

Edwards, Bill & Mike Carwile. *Standard Encyclopedia of Pressed Glass.* Paducah, Kentucky: Collector Books, 2000.

Hansen, Susan. Personal conversations. New York. Avon Products, Inc. 2002.

Hastin, Bud. *Avon Products and California Perfume Company Collectors Encyclopedia.* Kansas City: Bud Hastin, 1998.

Huxford, Bob and Sharon. *Flea Market Trader.* Paducah, Kentucky: Collector Books, 2002.

Huxford, Bob and Sharon. *Garage Sale and Flea Market Annual.* Paducah, Kentucky: Collector Books, 2003.

McCain, Mollie. *Collectors Encyclopedia of Pattern Glass.* Paducah, Kentucky: Collector Books, 1992.

Metz, Alize. *Early American Pattern Glass.* Columbus, Ohio: Spencer-Walker Press, 1960.

*Western World Handbook and Price Guide to Avon Collectibles.* Pleasant Hill, CA: Western World Publishing, 1985.

Wheaton Glass. Archival Material. Millville, New Jersey: Wheaton Glass, 1975 - 1993.

Zimmerman, Curtis. Personal Conversations. Millville, New Jersey: Wheaton USA, 2002.